BARRON'S BOOK NOTES

WILLIAM FAULKNER'S

As I Lay Dying

BY

Eric F. Oatman
Editor, *Scholastic Update*
Scholastic Inc.

SERIES COORDINATOR

Murray Bromberg
Principal, Wang High School of Queens
Holliswood, New York

Past President
High School Principals Association of New York City

BARRON'S EDUCATIONAL SERIES, INC.
Woodbury, New York • London • Toronto • Sydney

ACKNOWLEDGMENTS

Our thanks to Milton Katz and Julius Liebb for their advisory
assistance on the *Book Notes* series.

© Copyright 1985 by Barron's Educational Series, Inc.

All inquiries should be addressed to:
Barron's Educational Series, Inc.
113 Crossways Park Drive
Woodbury, New York 11797

Library of Congress Catalog Card No. 85-3955

International Standard Book No. 0-8120-3502-X

Library of Congress Cataloging in Publication Data

Oatman, Eric F.
  William Faulkner's As I lay dying.

  (Barron's book notes)
  Bibliography: p. 120
  Summary: A guide to reading "As I Lay Dying" with a
critical and appreciative mind encouraging analysis of
plot, style, form, and structure. Also includes
background on the author's life and times, sample tests,
term paper suggestions, and a reading list.
    1. Faulkner, William, 1897-1962. As I lay dying.
  [1. Faulkner, William, 1897-1962. As I lay dying.
  2. American literature—History and criticism]
  I. Faulkner, William, 1897-1962. As I lay dying.
  II. Title. III. Series.
PS3511.A86A866 1985   813'.52   85-3955
ISBN 0-8120-3502-X

CONTENTS

HOW TO USE THIS BOOK

You have to know how to approach literature in order to get the most out of it. This *Barron's Book Notes* volume follows a plan based on methods used by some of the best students to read a work of literature.

Begin with the guide's section on the author's life and times. As you read, try to form a clear picture of the author's personality, circumstances, and motives for writing the work. This background usually will make it easier for you to hear the author's tone of voice, and follow where the author is heading.

Then go over the rest of the introductory material—such sections as those on the plot, characters, setting, themes, and style of the work. Underline, or write down in your notebook, particular things to watch for, such as contrasts between characters and repeated literary devices. At this point, you may want to develop a system of symbols to use in marking your text as you read. (Of course, you should only mark up a book you own, not one that belongs to another person or a school.) Perhaps you will want to use a different letter for each character's name, a different number for each major theme of the book, a different color for each important symbol or literary device. Be prepared to mark up the pages of your book as you read. Put your marks in the margins so you can find them again easily.

Now comes the moment you've been waiting for—the time to start reading the work of literature. You may want to put aside your *Barron's Book Notes* volume until you've read the work all the way through. Or you may want to alternate, reading the *Book Notes* analysis of each section as soon as you have finished reading the corresponding part of the original. Before you move on, reread crucial passages you don't fully understand. (Don't take this guide's analysis for granted—make up your own mind as to what the work means.)

Once you've finished the whole work of literature, you may want to review it right away, so you can firm up your ideas about what it means. You may want to leaf through the book concentrating on passages you marked in reference to one character or one theme. This is also a good time to reread the *Book Notes* introductory material, which pulls together insights on specific topics.

When it comes time to prepare for a test or to write a paper, you'll already have formed ideas about the work. You'll be able to go back through it, refreshing your memory as to the author's exact words and perspective, so that you can support your opinions with evidence drawn straight from the work. Patterns will emerge, and ideas will fall into place; your essay question or term paper will almost write itself. Give yourself a dry run with one of the sample tests in the guide. These tests present both multiple-choice and essay questions. An accompanying section gives answers to the multiple-choice questions as well as suggestions for writing the essays. If you have to select a term paper topic, you may choose one from the list of suggestions in this book. This guide also provides you with a reading list, to help you when you start research for a term paper, and a selection of provocative comments by critics, to spark your thinking before you write.

THE AUTHOR AND HIS TIMES

No one who knew William Faulkner in high school would have voted him "most likely to succeed." He dropped out in the eleventh grade. "I never did like school," he said, "and I stopped going as soon as I got big enough to play hooky and not be caught at it."

Failure seemed attached to him like a tin can. His girlfriend married a man whose prospects were better than Faulkner's. The U.S. Army Air Corps wouldn't take him during World War I—he was too short.

In his twenties, he seemed incapable of applying himself to anything. He went to the University of Mississippi, did miserably in English, and quit after a year. Though he managed to get a job running the university's post office, he was so incompetent he was forced to resign. He was even removed as the local scoutmaster because he drank too much. The litany of his shortcomings stretches on: his almost paralyzing shyness, his inability to write memorable poetry, his years as a problem drinker.

And yet, this "failure" produced 90 short stories, 19 novels, and a play that was performed on Broadway. In 1950 he won the Nobel Prize for Literature, the highest recognition any writer can get. Today, he is considered one of the greatest writers the United States has ever produced.

How did this happen? A complete answer would have to take into account Faulkner's special gifts as a writer, developed over a long period of apprenticeship. *As I Lay Dying*, his fifth published novel, will give you an excellent chance to appreciate those gifts and his unique view of the world. That view stems, partly, from what critics call the Southern Tradition—the myths about the South as a defeated nation that he shared with other Southerners of his time.

Growing Up   William Cuthbert Falkner (he added the *u* when he became a published writer) was born in New Albany, Mississippi, on September 25, 1897. For the first four years of his life, he lived in Ripley, a nearby town whose cemetery is dominated by a statue of Faulkner's great-grandfather, Colonel William Clark Falkner. Faulkner never knew his great-grandfather—he had died in 1889. But Old Colonel Falkner, as he was called, remained a legendary figure to his descendants.

After the Civil War, Colonel Falkner refused to lick his wounds. He built a railroad, became rich, and wrote several novels, one of them a best-seller. He was shot and killed in Ripley's town square by his former partner in the railroad venture.

The Old Colonel's son, John, was a lawyer and a banker. When John's son Murry and his wife moved to Oxford in northern Mississippi, they already had three sons: William, who was four; Murry, three; and John, just one. A fourth boy, Dean, would be born in 1907. Some readers think that Faulkner's growing up with three brothers may have helped him work out the intricate relationships of the four brothers in *As I Lay Dying*.

William and John were old enough to be dazzled by Oxford, a county seat of some 1800 people. The electric street lamps—the first they had ever seen—were especially marvelous. Toward the end of *As*

I Lay Dying, the young boy Vardaman visits a town very much like Oxford, giving Faulkner the chance to re-create the sense of wonder the arc lamps gave him in his childhood.

Faulkner's mother, an amateur artist, tried to inspire in her sons a love of learning. There was, of course, no television or radio then, and silent movies became popular late in Faulkner's childhood. So, during the evenings, the family read a lot. Mrs. Falkner introduced her children to some of the great American and European writers.

Mrs. Falkner, a Baptist, took care of their religious education, too. William never had much use for organized religion. But he believed in God and Christian values, and he read the Bible regularly for pleasure. *As I Lay Dying* contains many references to the Old and New Testaments. Several of the novel's characters reflect Faulkner's understanding of the way Christianity shaped the views of the people he grew up among.

Faulkner seemed to lose all interest in schooling when he got to high school. "He gazed out the windows and answered the simplest question with 'I don't know,' " a classmate remembered. He was an outsider, often lost in daydreams like Darl, the poetic, brooding brother in *As I Lay Dying* whose neighbors thought him odd.

He quit school in December, 1914, then returned the next fall to the eleventh grade (the last grade his school offered) so that he could play football. When the season ended, he quit school for good and went to work as a clerk in his grandfather's bank.

The Southern Tradition   The South—as a region and a state of mind—plays a very important part in Faulkner's work. The South was defeated in the

Civil War and occupied for twelve years afterward by Federal troops. Many of the white Southerners who had supported the Confederacy were unable to accept the harsh facts of defeat. Their children—and their children's children, people like Faulkner—were steeped in the myths of the Old South. They heard again and again of the chivalry, heroism, and honor of its defenders. Like the regional dialects that Faulkner uses in *As I Lay Dying*, the subject of a ravaged homeland was a part of the tradition that these writers inherited.

But the South was changing during Faulkner's youth. Its political leaders were changing, too. Descendants of the aristocratic families of the Old South were losing power. They were being replaced by men who drew their strength from the new class of businessmen or from poor white farmers who feared that they were being left behind.

Faulkner wasn't sure what to make of the upheaval going on around him. He tried to come to terms with it. Like Bayard Sartoris, the main character in Faulkner's third novel, *Sartoris*, he wasn't sure there was a place for him in this New South.

Faulkner would deal directly with these themes in several of his books. In *As I Lay Dying*, he approaches them indirectly, suggesting conflicts between the hill farmers—the "rednecks"—and the townspeople.

Here and there in *As I Lay Dying*, you'll see him betray a certain affection for the myths of the Old South. The character who comes closest to being a hero, Jewel, is a man of action, and he's often mounted on a horse like the South's gallant defenders during the Civil War. And the Bundrens, who hold center stage in *As I Lay Dying*, are a sort of proud guerrilla band fighting their own rear guard action against a powerful enemy.

Literary Apprenticeship Faulkner wrote little more than poetry before leaving Oxford in 1918 to join the Royal Flying Corps in Canada. Most of that poetry, as Faulkner later acknowledged, wasn't very good. "I'm a failed poet," he once told an interviewer. "Maybe every novelist wants to write poetry first, finds he can't, and then tries the short story, which is the most demanding form after poetry. And, failing at that, only then does he take up novel writing."

Faulkner didn't take up novel writing until he went to New Orleans in 1925, after he was allowed to resign from his job as a postmaster near Oxford. In New Orleans he made friends with the novelist Sherwood Anderson, who encouraged him to write fiction.

Faulkner's first novel, *Soldiers' Pay*, was published in 1926. It is the story of an American soldier who returns home to Georgia to die of the wounds received in World War I. His second book, *Mosquitoes*, published in 1927, makes fun of the artistic and social circles he knew in New Orleans. Light on plot and heavy on hollow talk, the novel embodies a theme that Faulkner explores in *As I Lay Dying*: the uselessness of words when separated from action.

In 1928, Faulkner wrote *Sartoris*, which told of the decay of a proud Southern family much like his own. The book is set in Jefferson, a fictitious town in Mississippi that resembles Oxford. Jefferson is the Bundren family's destination in *As I Lay*

Dying. In that novel, published in 1930, Faulkner for the first time gives a name—Yoknapatawpha—to the county of which Jefferson is the political center. (For the derivation of the name, see Note in section 45 of The Story section.)

While *Sartoris* was being readied for publication in January, 1929, Faulkner wrote *The Sound and the Fury.* Many readers think that this second novel in the Yoknapatawpha saga is Faulkner's masterpiece. It is a study of the collapse of another proud Southern family, the Compsons. A difficult book, it tells its story in three stream-of-consciousness styles Faulkner had learned from reading the Irish writer James Joyce. Faulkner told the story first through the eyes of an idiot, then through the eyes of two brothers.

Convinced that he would never make any money writing, he returned in his next book to a more conventional way of presenting material. He conceived of *Sanctuary* as a "potboiler"—a salable mix of sex and violence. When it was published in 1931, it became a best-seller.

Before *Sanctuary* came out, however, Faulkner wrote and published *As I Lay Dying.* Its plot is relatively straightforward, the story of a poor family's journey from the hills of Yoknapatawpha County to Jefferson to bury one of its members. But the story is told in a way that is anything but straightforward. Like *The Sound and the Fury,* the novel has no single narrator. Instead, it has 15 narrators—family members and outsiders—who piece together a funeral journey in 59 unnumbered sections. The result is a tour de force, a work of art that displays Faulkner's incredible technical skill as a writer. Even more incredible is the fact that he wrote the book in just 47 days!

That's a story in itself. In June 1929, he had married Estelle Oldham Franklin, a girlfriend who had turned her back on him 11 years earlier. He took a job as a supervisor at the University of Mississippi's power plant. It was night work and consisted of firing the boilers with coal until about 11 P.M., when the students went to bed. There was no more work to do until 4 A.M., so each night Faulkner wrote a chapter or more of *As I Lay Dying* on a wheelbarrow he had turned into a desk.

A quarter century later, Faulkner recalled the experience:

> Sometimes technique charges in and takes command of the dream before the writer himself can get his hands on it. That is tour de force and the finished work is simply a matter of fitting bricks neatly together, since the writer knows probably every single word right to the end before he puts the first one down. This happened with *As I Lay Dying.* It was not easy. No honest work is. It was simple in that all the material was already at hand. It took me just about six weeks. . . .

Faulkner took the novel's title from a line in Homer's *Odyssey:* "As I lay dying the woman with the dog's eyes would not close my eyelids for me as I descended into Hades." The line is spoken by the dead King Agamemnon. Odysseus meets him in the underworld and is moved by his story. The kind had been killed by his wife Clytemnestra and her lover, Aegisthus. As he died, Clytemnestra— "the woman with the dog's eyes"—demonstrated her heartlessness by refusing to close his eyes and so ease his descent into the underworld. With Faulkner, you can get into trouble trying to make literal sense of titles. Still, when you finish the novel,

you may want to return to the title and try to make
your own sense of it.

Once you get into the novel, you should have
no trouble enjoying it. "Of all Faulkner's novels,"
the critic Irving Howe said, "*As I Lay Dying* is the
warmest, the kindliest and most affectionate. . . .
In no other work is he so receptive to people, so
ready to take and love them, to hear them out and
record their turns of idiom, their melodies of
speech."

Faulkner had more than three decades of work
ahead of him after he finished *As I Lay Dying*. In
1930, he began contributing short stories to na-
tional magazines. He published thirteen of them
in book form in 1931, the year he gained some
fame—or notoriety—with *Sanctuary*.

Unlike *Sanctuary*, *As I Lay Dying* and *The Sound
and the Fury* failed to reach wide audiences. When
As I Lay Dying appeared in October 1930 reviewers
generally praised it, even when annoyed. But
readers found Faulkner's stream of consciousness
techniques hard going and the world of Yoknapatawpha County as foreign as Mars.

In 1932, Faulkner couldn't sell the magazine rights
to a more conventional novel, *Light in August*. So
he took a job writing film scripts in Hollywood. He
would write films, off and on, for the next 22
years. None of the films was especially memorable. Writing them kept him from his family for
long stretches. Yet the movies helped him pay his
bills.

He wrote a succession of fine novels after *Light
in August*—*Pylon* (1935), *Absalom, Absalom!* (1936),
and *The Unvanquished* (1938) among them. During
most of the 1940s, however, it was hard to find
any of his novels in bookstores.

The Nobel Prize for Literature he won in 1950 changed all that. His publishers put his books back in print. And although his great creative period had ended in 1938, even the weaker novels he now wrote sold well.

Faulkner died of a heart attack in 1962, a little more than 32 years after he wrote *As I Lay Dying*. Some years before he died, he recalled the goal he had in mind when he wrote the novel: "I said, I am going to write a book by which, at a pinch, I can stand or fall if I never touch ink again."

As his reader, you are the final judge of his effort. Did he succeed in his aim of writing a book that his reputation could rest on?

THE NOVEL

The Plot

Addie, a schoolteacher, marries Anse Bundren, a tall man with a humped back who has a farm in the hills of Yoknapatawpha County. They have a child, Cash, who makes Addie feel less alone and whom she loves.

Her contentment with one child is shattered when she finds herself pregnant with her second child, Darl. She feels that Anse has tricked her with words of love, which she is sure he cannot feel. In revenge, she secures a promise she knows will be nearly impossible to keep. She makes Anse promise to bury her next to her relatives 40 miles away in Jefferson, the county seat, when she dies.

One summer, Addie has a brief, passionate affair with Whitfield, a preacher. They have a son, Jewel, whom Anse raises as his own. To make amends to Anse for her unfaithfulness, she has two other children, Dewey Dell and Vardaman.

When Vardaman is eight or nine, Addie lies dying on her corn-shuck mattress. Outside her window, Cash, now a 29-year-old carpenter, carefully fashions her coffin as a gesture of love. While the Tulls—neighbors—are visiting, Darl convinces Jewel to take a trip with him to pick up a load of lumber. Darl knows that Jewel is Addie's favorite child. The trip for lumber is a contrivance—Darl's way of keeping Jewel from his mother's bedside when she dies.

Their absence with the family's wagon presents a problem. In the July heat, dead bodies decompose rapidly. A wheel breaks, and before Darl and

Jewel can replace it, bring the wagon home, and load Addie's body onto it for the trip to Jefferson, three days have passed.

By this time, heavy rains have flooded the Yoknapatawpha River and washed out all the bridges that cross it. The Bundrens travel past the Tulls' house to the Samsons', then back to the Tulls' again to ford the river at what had been a shallow place before the flood.

The river is vicious. The Bundrens' mules drown. The wagon tips over, dumping Cash and breaking his leg. Jewel, on horseback, manages to keep the wagon and its load from drifting downstream.

They stop at the Amstids' on the other side of the river. Anse trades Jewel's horse and Cash's eight dollars—he had been saving for a wind-up phonograph—for a new mule team.

To reach Jefferson, the Bundrens have to drive out of the county to Mottson. Addie's rotting body outrages the townspeople. The Bundrens buy a dime's worth of cement to make a cast for Cash's leg. Dewey Dell, who is pregnant, tries and fails to buy some abortion pills in the local drugstore.

They spend the night at the Gillespies' farm. Darl sets fire to the barn where Addie's body is stored in an effort to spare his mother more degradation. However, Jewel saves her coffin with a heroic act. Dewey Dell, who hates Darl because he knows she is pregnant, realizes that Darl set the fire and tells the Gillespies.

The Bundrens reach Jefferson nine days after Addie's death. They dig her grave with borrowed shovels and then get on with their own lives. They commit Darl to the state insane asylum rather than pay the Gillespies for a new barn. A dishonest drugstore clerk takes advantage of Dewey Dell, who fails to get the abortion pills she wanted. Anse takes money from Dewey Dell, buys a set of false teeth, and marries a "duck-shaped" woman.

The Characters

Faulkner provides you with two basic perspectives on the characters, allowing you to view them through their own interior monologues and through the eyes of others. You must sort through the different views to arrive at your own understanding of the Bundrens and their neighbors.

What follows is an exploration of the 15 characters whose interior monologues make up the novel. The seven Bundrens are presented first. The numbers after the characters' names refer to the sections they narrate. Faulkner didn't number the sections. They are numbered here to help you match your copy of the novel with the section-by-section discussion in this guide. (See the Note on Numbering the Monologues at the beginning of The Story section.)

THE BUNDRENS
Anse Bundren [9, 26, 28]
Anse is a hill farmer who inherited his parents' farm just south of the Yoknapatawpha River, which crosses the southern end of Yoknapatawpha County. A lazy man, he has convinced himself that if he ever sweats, he will die. He is so ineffectual when confronted with obstacles that his sons have to make many of his decisions for him.

Yet he seems to mean well. When Addie dies, his grief appears genuine, although he can express it only clumsily. In at least one place—while staying at Samson's—his resolve to honor Addie's wish to be buried in Jefferson wavers. But in general he sticks to the promise he made to her 28 years earlier, at Darl's birth, and insists on taking her body to Jefferson, which he has not visited for 12 years.

Selfishness is one of his major motivations, and he is adept at deceiving himself. Some readers see Anse as a comic figure—a sad clown. Others view him as a villain, able to act only from selfish motives. But to people such as Addie, he's a "dead" person, substituting empty words for experience.

You should try to see whether Anse grows or otherwise changes during the course of the action. Study his words at the end of the book to determine whether he has gained insights into himself or anyone else since he first appeared in section 3.

Addie Bundren [40]

Though Anse's wife, Addie, is given only one monologue, her presence, even in death, dominates the novel. Born and raised in Jefferson, her father taught her that the purpose of living is to prepare for death. Her parents were dead and she was teaching school when she met Anse. She married him—"I took Anse," she said—in hopes of making the sort of intense, violent contact with another person that would give her life meaning.

Anse couldn't provide that experience. He could only talk about it—not the same thing at all, Addie points out. Cash, her firstborn, does penetrate the circle of solitude around her, and she loves him. Her attitude toward her children, whether love, hostility, or indifference, helps them define themselves and their response to her death.

About ten years after Darl's birth, she has a passionate affair with a preacher named Whitfield, who

fathers her favorite son, Jewel. She makes amends
to Anse by having two more children.

Despite her negative qualities, Addie may be
visualized as a life force. She craves passionate en-
counters, violations of her "aloneness." Some
readers have identified her with the myth of Demeter, the major goddess of fertility, and her
daughter, Persephone, goddess of spring and thus
also of fertility.

Other readers stress the barrenness of her life—
her father's destructive teachings, her loneliness,
her vengefulness, her rejection of Darl and her indifference toward Dewey Dell and Vardaman. These
readers feel that Faulkner may be turning the Demeter-Persephone myth on its head, making Addie in death as well as in life a sort of goddess of
*in*fertility.

Cash Bundren [18, 22, 38, 53, 59]
Cash, at 29 or 30 Addie's oldest son, is a carpenter.
His name is short for Cassius. His mother loved
him, and he returns that love, painstakingly crafting her coffin outside her window in the opening
scenes. A recognizable country type, his unexpected responses—to pain, for example, and to a
question about the height of his fall from a church
roof—are a source of humor. At the end of the
book, his insights into the family relationships and
Darl's sanity reveal him to be the wisest of the
Bundrens, and perhaps the one most changed by
the journey.

His lameness suggests to some readers a parallel
with Hephaestus (also known as Vulcan or Mul-
ciber), the Greek god of fire. Hephaestus was a
kindly, peace-loving god, patron of handicrafts.

Though lame, he made weapons and furnishings for the other gods.

Darl Bundren [1, 3, 5, 10, 12, 17, 21, 23, 25, 27, 32, 34, 37, 42, 46, 48, 50, 52, 57]

Darl, about 28 years old, narrates a third of the book and is easily the most perceptive of the Bundren children. A sort of mad poet, he is a type that always intrigued Faulkner and with whom he often identified. The neighbors consider him odd. He is clairvoyant, that is, able to understand unspoken thoughts and to describe scenes he doesn't witness.

Addie's rejection of him is the central fact of his life. His rivalry with Jewel, Addie's favorite son, is evident on the first page and continues to the end of the book. His sensitivity stems, at least in part, some readers think, from the wounds inflicted by his mother's rejection of him.

Why he sets fire to the barn is, like his sanity, a matter of debate. Many readers believe that he wanted to end the journey by burning Addie's decomposing corpse—perhaps as an act of love, "to hide her away from the sight of man." Others see his setting of the fire as a mark of insanity, justifying his being committed to an asylum at Jackson at the end of the book. You will have an opportunity to offer your own explanation as you learn more about Darl.

Jewel Bundren [4]

Jewel, Addie's son by Whitfield, is 18 years old. Like Pearl, the product of Hester Prynne's adulterous affair in Nathaniel Hawthorne's novel *The Scarlet Letter*, Jewel's name is a symbol of the value his mother places on him. The favoritism that Addie showed him is responsible for the antagonism between him and Darl.

A blend of inarticulateness and action, Jewel personifies Addie's preference for experience over words. He is always in motion. He expresses himself best through actions. When he verbalizes his love for Addie—in his single monologue—he does so with a violent fantasy about hurling down stones on outsiders. Elsewhere, he expresses his love for her through deeds, not words.

His relationship with his horse is equally intense. Like the Greek god Dionysus, with whom some readers associate him, Jewel is both virile and cruel. (See the Note in Chapter 1 of The Story section for further discussion of Jewel as Dionysus.)

Dewey Dell Bundren [7, 14, 30, 58]

Dewey Dell, Addie's fourth child, is 17. Unable to complete a thought, she seems at times like a mindless animal. By her name and actions, Faulkner identifies her with the earth and with fertility—a "wet seed wild in the hot blind earth." Perhaps because of her mother's indifference to her, she seems unmoved by Addie's death. She is pregnant and eager to go to Jefferson because she hopes to buy abortion pills there.

Dewey Dell has a vindictive side. She hates Darl for knowing that she is pregnant and seeks revenge by betraying him. With Vardaman, however, she shows maternal feelings.

Some readers associate Dewey Dell with Persephone, the goddess of spring and queen of the underworld in Greek myth. They point out, however, that once again Faulkner may be turning the Demeter-Persephone myth on its head. By seeking an abortion, this goddess of fertility is denying her own powers.

Vardaman Bundren [13, 15, 19, 24, 35, 44, 47]

Eight or nine years old, Vardaman is the son Addie gave Anse to "replace the child I robbed him of." She is looking at him when she dies. He is so traumatized by her death, he at first blames Doc Peabody for it, then confuses Addie in his mind with a huge fish he caught the afternoon she died.

OTHER CHARACTERS

Whitfield [41]

Addie's lover and Jewel's father, Whitfield is the preacher who heads for the Bundrens' farm when he hears that Addie is dying. Perhaps fearing Addie will confess their brief affair on her deathbed, he intends to admit the transgression himself.

Addie dies before Whitfield arrives, and he decides that God will accept his intention to confess in place of the actual confession. His monologue, full of empty religiosity of the sort Addie detested, suggests that Addie may have misjudged him some nineteen years earlier.

He presides over her funeral. The impression he gives Tull—that his voice is not part of his body—calls attention to the disparity between his words and actions.

Vernon Tull [8, 16, 20, 31, 33, 36]

Vernon Tull—or just Tull—is a neighbor who lives four miles from the Bundrens. You can trust his observations because, unlike his wife Cora, he never judges what he sees, he merely reports.

Try as he might, he can't *not* help Anse. "I done

holp him so much already I cant quit now," he says.

Cora Tull [2, 6, 39]

Cora, like Addie a former teacher, is a well-meaning woman who lectures Addie on the need to repent her sins. Despite her empty piety, some see Cora as a sympathetic character, one that Faulkner makes you care about. She doesn't have much use for the Bundrens but believes, as her religion teaches, that it is her duty to help her fellow mortals.

Doc Peabody [11, 51]

Seventy years old and weighing more than 200 pounds, Lucius Quintus Peabody (Faulkner gives the full name in his novel *Sartoris*) is, like Tull, a reliable narrator. Early in the novel, he makes a house call to the Bundrens' to see Addie. He introduces one of the novel's themes—that death is felt not by those who die but by their survivors. Toward the end of the novel, in Jefferson, he treats Cash's broken leg.

Samson [29]

Samson owns a farm eight miles from the Bundrens'. When Anse and his family are unable to cross the river by bridge, they stay at Samson's overnight. His firmness tempered by understanding, Samson suggests that they bury Addie in nearby New Hope. But Anse, prodded by Dewey Dell, ignores the advice. Samson's wife, Rachel—an emotional and, to Samson, unpredictable woman—is outraged by Addie's treatment.

Armstid [43]

Armstid, a farmer on the north side of the Yoknapatawpha River, lends Jewel his mules so that the Bundrens can move their wagon away from the river. The Bundrens stay at Armstid's farm one night, and down the road from it a second night. One of the most generous people the Bundrens meet, Armstid offers them more aid—food, lodging, and the extended use of his team—than they are willing to accept.

Moseley [45]

Moseley runs the drugstore in Mottson. A righteous man, he refuses to sell Dewey Dell anything to abort her child. He reports the townspeople's view of the rest of the Bundren clan, who were waiting outside a hardware store while Darl bought cement for Cash's cast.

Skeet MacGowan [55]

MacGowan, a druggist's assistant in Jefferson, takes advantage of Dewey Dell's naïveté and seduces her.

Other Elements
SETTING

As I Lay Dying takes place in or just outside Yoknapatawpha County, the "apocryphal kingdom" in northern Mississippi where 15 of Faulkner's 19 novels are set. Faulkner never disguised the fact that he modeled Yoknapatawpha after his own Lafayette County, where he lived for most of his life. Jefferson, Yoknapatawpha's county seat, is much like Oxford, Faulkner's hometown.

Yoknapatawpha is sparsely populated. Faulkner once put its population at 15,611, and its land area at 2400 square miles. The Bundrens' closest neighbors in the pine hills, the Tulls, live four miles away. One of the themes of *As I Lay Dying* is isolation—the isolation even of people who are united in a common effort. The distance between the farms in Yoknapatawpha's hill country advances that theme. The Tulls, Samsons, Armstids, and Bundrens are all part of the same community, yet each family operates within its own orbit, and within that orbit each individual lives locked in the "cell" of his own consciousness.

The Bundrens' journey to Jefferson takes them from the world of farmers and woodsmen to the world of storekeepers, mechanics, doctors and lawyers. The worlds are as different as day and night. Indeed, Faulkner suggests that the Yoknapatawpha River is a dividing line as significant to the Bundrens as the mythological River Styx was to the ancient Greeks. The River Styx, in Greek mythology, separated the world of the living from the world of the dead. Conflict between town and country folk is a motif that crops up throughout the novel.

Finding obstacles to put in the Bundrens' path wasn't difficult. "I simply imagined a group of people and subjected them to the simple universal natural catastrophes, which are flood and fire," Faulkner said in 1956. Rain and flood dominate the first two thirds of the book, adding to the Bundrens' stress and enabling Faulkner to study their response to crisis.

THEMES

Here is a list of the major themes that readers have found in *As I Lay Dying*. You will have a chance to explore them further in the section-by-section discussion of the novel. Some of these themes are contradictory. It is up to you to sort

out those you think are valid from those you think
invalid.

1. DEATH SHAPES LIFE

Addie, in death, motivates the living. She causes
her family to bear the struggle of the journey to
Jefferson. Her different attitudes toward her children dictate their different responses to her death
and prompt one—Jewel—to perform feats of heroism. The rivalry between Jewel and Darl continues long after Addie's death. Even her decaying
corpse motivates the living—to flee.

2. LIFE IS ABSURD—A JOURNEY WITH NO MEANING

The purpose of the journey, from Addie's point
of view, is revenge. But Anse isn't allowed to understand that. Nor is he perceptive enough to understand that the journey is senseless. He could
have buried Addie at New Hope and bought false
teeth another day. This interpretation was popular
in the 1950s, especially among French Existential-
ists, members of a philosophical movement that
holds the universe to be absurd.

3. HUMANS HAVE AN OBLIGATION TO BE INVOLVED WITH OTHERS

Some readers interpret Addie's longing for intense personal contact—her "duty to the alive, to
the terrible blood"—as support for this theme. Such
involvement with others gives meaning to existence. The help the Bundrens are given by their
neighbors and the help they give each other demonstrate the importance of involvement.

4. ALL HUMANS LIVE IN SOLITUDE AND SOLIDARITY AT THE SAME TIME

We live in our own cells even while acting in
unison with others to achieve a common goal—a

goal as simple as moving a body about 40 miles to a cemetery. The 59 interior monologues that make up the novel are clear demonstrations of the cells in which individuals live. "Man is free and he is responsible, terribly responsible," Faulkner told an interviewer in 1959. "His tragedy is the impossibility—or at least the tremendous difficulty—of communication. But man keeps on trying endlessly to express himself and make contact with other human beings."

5. LANGUAGE IS VANITY WHILE ACTION—EVEN "SINFUL" ACTION—IS THE TEST OF LIFE

This is a theme of great importance to Addie, for whom words are "just a shape to fill a lack." "Words go straight up in a thin line, quick and harmless," she says, while "doing goes along the earth, clinging to it. . . ." In various ways, Anse, Cora, and Whitfield exemplify the emptiness of words when compared with action. On the other hand, the most inarticulate character in the novel, Jewel, is all motion. He expresses himself through action, not words.

6. TRUTH IS ELUSIVE, SINCE FACTS ARE SUBJECTIVE

Each of the novel's 15 narrators has a perspective on reality that may or may not be accurate. Is Darl sane or insane? Is Vardaman's mother a fish? Is Addie's sin, as Cora says, the sin of pride, and the log that struck the wagon "the hand of God"? Does Anse have some feeling, a lot of feeling, or no feeling toward Addie? Since Faulkner provides no narrator to help you sift through the various characters' perceptions, you are left to draw your own conclusions.

Readers have also identified several secondary themes in *As I Lay Dying*. Among them are the following.

1. THE CONFLICT BETWEEN THE POOR WHITE FARMERS AND THE TOWNSPEOPLE

These two groups are at odds throughout the novel, from the "rich town" lady's rejection of Cora's cakes to Dewey Dell's seduction by the slick druggist's assistant in Jefferson.

2. DARL'S PREOCCUPATION WITH JEWEL

Darl, the unwanted son, is obsessed with Jewel, the favorite son, from the first sentence of the novel almost to the end.

3. THE POWER TO ACT

Some characters have this power, some don't. After reading *As I Lay Dying*, you might want to rank the characters according to their ability to act. Most readers would place Jewel at the head of the list, Anse at the bottom.

4. THE POWER TO LOVE

Some of the characters have this ability, some can only talk about it. Perhaps more than anyone, Addie and Jewel have this power—one which Jewel, by saving his mother twice, merges with his power to act. As the Bible would have it, he does "not love in word, neither in tongue; but in deed and in truth" (1 John 3:18).

5. THE ROLE OF SEX

It is a source of tension between men and women, an antidote to loneliness, and a method of achieving immortality. Addie lives on through her children and through children who, like Dewey Dell's, are yet unborn.

STYLE

Faulkner is a difficult writer. His style—the way he expresses things—is often closer to poetry than to prose. Like a poet, he tries to capture the emotion of an experience as well as the experience itself.

Faulkner deliberately withholds meaning to keep his options open, to keep his story in motion. In the opening section, for instance, he describes an odd competition between Darl and Jewel but never tells you whether it really is a competition or what it's all about. You have to read many more sections before you can make sense of that first one. In Addie's section [40], her thoughts jump from experience (her history) to ideas (her theory of the distance between words and deeds) and to unanchored impressions ("the terrible blood, the red bitter blood boiling through the land") whose meaning you must almost guess at.

The beauty of *As I Lay Dying* is that its structure permits Faulkner to create numerous voices. Dewey Dell's breathy rush of unfinished thoughts is one distinct voice. Vernon Tull's folk dialect is another, and MacGowan's wise-guy patter is still another. The repetitive structure of Whitfield's monologue [41] mimics Psalms in the Old Testament. In large part, this demonstration of Faulkner's virtuosity in handling a number of voices comfortably is what people are talking about when they call *As I Lay Dying* a tour de force, an expression of an author's technical mastery.

Keep an eye out for Faulkner's startling use of

imagery. It would be useful for you to jot down the first ten images that make an impression on you and ask yourself why they are memorable. Much of Faulkner's imagery is visual (pertaining to sight). But his imagery can also be *olfactory* (pertaining to smell), *tactile* (touch), *auditory* (hearing), *gustatory* (taste), and even abstract in its appeal to the intellect.

The lyric description of drinking water from a cedar bucket [section 3] provides examples of these forms of imagery. "Warmish-cool, with a faint taste like the hot July wind in cedar trees smells" mixes gustatory, tactile, and olfactory imagery in one sentence. A paragraph later, Faulkner mixes auditory and tactile imagery: "I could lie with my shirt-tail up, hearing them asleep, feeling myself without touching myself, feeling the cool silence blowing. . . ."

It's Faulkner's abstract imagery that may give you the most trouble. "I cannot love my mother because I have no mother," Darl says in section 21. "Jewel's mother is a horse."

Faulkner makes imaginative uses of figures of speech in which one thing is described in terms of another (*metaphor*) or in which one thing is likened to another (*simile*). In section 21, Jewel shapes a horse in his imagination "in a rigid stoop like a hawk, hook-winged" (simile). Darl describes the floating log that topples the wagon "upright . . . like Christ" (simile), and later Cora calls the log "the hand of God" (metaphor). Extending the Christ image, Darl speaks metaphorically of "the bearded head of the rearing log." Earlier, Faulkner uses metaphor to suggest that Jewel's horse is Pegasus—"enclosed by a glittering maze of hooves as by an illusion of wings." What he is doing here, as elsewhere, is implying analogies between his characters and those from ancient myth.

In a consideration of style, it's important to remember that all the action is described through interior monologues—thought processes presented as speech. Interior monologues play three key roles. They (1) move the action forward, (2) reveal the characters' private thoughts, and (3) comment on what the other characters do. They also permit some of Faulkner's characters to use, in their unspoken thoughts, some highly sophisticated language. "The lantern," Darl observes in section 17, ". . . sheds a feeble and sultry glare upon the trestles and the boards and the adjacent earth." In section 13, the young boy Vardaman sees "the dark . . . resolving him out of his integrity, into an unrelated scattering of components." When they speak aloud, however, these characters are country folk through-and-through. "You mind that ere fish," Vardaman tells Tull.

The folk dialect of Tull, Anse, and Cash seems to take some of the horror out of the journey. Tull describes Vardaman's boring holes through the lid of Addie's coffin: "When they taken the lid off they found that two of them had bored on into her face. If it's a judgment, it ain't right. . . ."

As one reader says, Faulkner "crosses farce with anguish" in *As I Lay Dying*. And a lot of the farce, or slapstick humor, is in the language—Faulkner's style.

POINT OF VIEW

As I Lay Dying is made up of a succession of first-person narratives, with the action seen and interpreted by fifteen characters. The narrators are sub-

jective—they convey their own feelings and
thoughts as well as report the action. None of them
is detached from the action for long.

Seven of the narrators are Bundrens, totally
caught up in the events and unable to make complete sense of them. Darl never ceases to try, however, and Cash gains some perspective at the end.

The other eight narrators are outsiders. Faulkner
uses them to show you how observers—some of
them neutral (Tull, Peabody, Samson, Armstid,
Moseley), some of them not so neutral (Cora,
Whitfield, MacGowan)—view the Bundrens.

Since all the narrators are wrapped up in the
action, you ought to question their reliability. Anse
says he is "beholden to no man," but we learn he
is. Cora is convinced that Jewel and Anse forced
Darl to leave his dying mother's bedside. She is
wrong. What you've got to do is test the narrators'
perceptions against each other, then draw your own
conclusions.

One of the major themes of the novel is that
because facts are subjective, truth is elusive. It's
not easy to make sense of the action with so many
competing points of view. You must sift the evidence and make up your own mind about what
happened and why.

Faulkner surely has an opinion of each character. But even when his characters are most vile—
when Anse, for example, takes Dewey Dell's
money, or MacGowan seduces her—Faulkner refuses to criticize them. He portrays his characters,
warts and all, with affection.

The use of multiple narrators is an effective substitute for an omniscient (all-knowing) narrator.
Omniscient narrators allow novelists to present
several perspectives on events. The fifteen narra-

tors in *As I Lay Dying* permit Faulkner—and you—
to work with fifteen perspectives.

FORM AND STRUCTURE

As I Lay Dying is divided into 59 soliloquies, or
interior monologues—the characters' thoughts ex-
pressed as if they were spoken. They are delivered
by 15 different people.

The basic plot and the controlling image of the
novel is that of a journey—in this case, the journey
from the Bundrens' home to the cemetery plot in
Jefferson. As some readers have pointed out, the
story echoes many of the well-known journeys in
history and myth. The story of Odysseus wander-
ing for years before he reaches home is suggested
by the novel's title, a quote from Homer's *Odyssey*.
Jason's quest for the Golden Fleece is another epic
voyage called to some reader's minds. Also, in 1290,
England's Edward I made a famous funeral journey from Nottinghamshire to London with his dead
queen, Eleanor of Castile.

Faulkner's story of a poor family's funeral journey wasn't intended to compete with those grand
tales. Yet they form the backdrop against which
Faulkner plays out his story.

For the most part, the story is told chronologi-
cally. It begins just before Addie's death and pro-
ceeds, after a three-day delay, with the tortuous
journey to Jefferson. Later, flashbacks fill in some
of the pieces that are missing from the puzzle of
the Bundrens' lives.

The novel's form is an expression of its content.
The characters work together and live together—
if not in the same house, at least in the same community. Yet their isolation from one another is al-

most total, and it is exemplified by the 59 monologues. For the most part, the fifteen soliloquists are unable to make meaningful contact with one another. They cannot penetrate each other's "aloneness."

The Story

Not numbering the 59 monologues is Faulkner's effective way of suggesting continuous action, but it makes any section-by-section discussion of the novel difficult. To eliminate that problem, you might want to number the monologues in your own copy of the novel to make it easier to match your text with the discussion that follows.

1. DARL

In this opening section, Faulkner carefully establishes the setting of *As I Lay Dying* and introduces you to one of the novel's central conflicts—the rivalry between Darl and his younger brother, Jewel. You also get your first impression of Darl's mind, another major focus of the novel.

NOTE: Avoiding Confusion Expect to be somewhat disoriented at the outset, much as you would be if you overheard a snippet of conversation between two strangers. You will find few identifying labels attached to the people named in this section. Yet, as the novel develops, the identities and motivations of each character will become clear through clues which Faulkner drops and which you, as a detective, must interpret.

As the story opens, Darl and Jewel are tramping silently across a cotton field toward their house. Faulkner doesn't tell you that they are brothers, or even how old they are. (Darl, you will learn much later, is about 28, and Jewel is about 18.) Faulkner does tell you that Jewel is a head taller than Darl and that, for some reason, they are rivals.

Their silent march is loaded with tension, as if the two were actually competing. Darl is 15 feet ahead of Jewel as the section opens. But when they reach the cotton house, exactly in the center of the field, Darl walks around it. Jewel, however, steps through it—in one window and out another—and emerges five feet ahead of Darl. They keep this pace all the way to the spring, where Jewel pauses for a drink.

Jewel has quit the race—if race it was. Darl continues on, and as he reaches the top of the path, he comes upon a carpenter named Cash. (Cash, we will learn, is at 29 the oldest of the four brothers.) Cash is making a coffin for someone named Addie Bundren. He is completely absorbed in his work, kneeling alongside the coffin to squint at the fit of two planks. Darl's words of admiration—"a good carpenter, Cash is"—suggests no rancor between these two. He walks by Cash up to the house, which holds (though we don't know it yet) the cause, and the object, of the rivalry between Darl and Jewel.

Various clues in the section make it clear that these are poor country people. The section also provides some insight into Jewel's character, or at least Darl's perception of it. He seems unsmiling and stiff, with a "wooden face" and the "gravity of a cigar store Indian . . . endued with life from the hips down." He seems undaunted by obstacles, too. He "steps in a single stride" through one window of the cotton house and exits, four strides later, out the other.

NOTE: Jewel and Imagery of Wood   Darl frequently describes Jewel with imagery of wood, here and elsewhere. Some readers think that in so doing, Faulkner is trying to associate Jewel with Dionysus, the Greek god of fertility and wine who was also a god of trees. Dionysus was conceived in the woods at Nemi. Jewel was also conceived in the woods, as you will learn in section 40.

Dionysus was both violent and cruel—two primitive characteristics that Jewel will exhibit in both thought and action. He was also very manly. Jewel's virility is hinted at with the reference to his being "endued with life from the hips down," and in section 8 it is suggested that he is somewhat of a ladies' man.

You can choose to ignore this interpretation. Most readers do. If you follow such parallels, however— even if they lead to dead ends—you will learn something about Faulkner's method of weaving references to ancient myth into his works. You'll learn more about this method in the discussion of sections 3 and 11.

Finally, the opening section gives you a glimpse of Darl's mind and of his special powers as an observer. He describes with geometric precision the setting of the silent race, almost as if he were in a helicopter looking down at the scene. The path runs "straight as a plumb-line" and goes around the "square" cotton house "at four soft right angles." He is aware of everything—the spaces between the coffin planks "yellow as gold" and the "chucking" sound of Cash's adze (a curved, handled tool used to dress timber and planks). He even knows what's going on *behind* him!

What sort of a person is Darl, judging from the way he sees things? Here, he will probably strike you as someone whose mind is uncluttered, despite its capacity to accumulate details. His vision seems absolutely clear. He appears to be an accurate reporter, someone whose perceptions you can trust.

Be careful, however. Darl will narrate almost a third of the book. As the novel progresses, he may not always appear rational and trustworthy.

NOTE: Tone and Comic Effects   Before leaving this opening section, assess its tone. Darl's attitude seems matter-of-fact, accepting. He doesn't criticize Jewel, or even comment on the tension between them. His entire tone is one of understanding and sincerity. He makes no obvious attempt at humor.

And yet, there's something gently comic about the whole scene. Most readers find themselves smiling at the silent march across the field, at Jewel's abrupt passage through the cotton house "still staring straight ahead," and at Darl's comment that "Addie Bundren could not want . . . a better box to lie in. It will give her confidence and comfort." If you find yourself smiling at these points, take a moment to ask yourself why.

---

2. CORA

This section introduces you to the Tull family—
Cora, her husband Vernon, and their daughters
Kate and Eula—and it gives you your first glimpse
of Addie Bundren. It also gives you, in Cora, a
look at the unfelt, shallow piety that, you learn
later, repulses Addie.

Though she is an object of humor, Cora has
characteristics that can draw you to her. "So I saved
out the eggs and baked yesterday," her monologue begins. She was baking, it turns out, in hopes
of selling cakes to a lady in town. But the lady
called off her party and Cora is stuck with her cakes.

Does the turn of events bother Cora? Her pride
is hurt ("They turned out real well") and so is her
pocketbook ("I could have used the money real
well"). But Cora, being Cora, refuses to admit to
any loss. The lady who made the order "ought to
taken those cakes anyway," Cora's daughter Kate
remarks—not once, but four times.

NOTE: Conflict Between Country and Town   A
recurring theme throughout *As I Lay Dying* is the
conflict between the hill people and those who live
in towns, especially Jefferson, the county seat. The
episode of the spurned cakes is the first instance
of this conflict. "Those rich town ladies can change
their minds. Poor folks cant," Kate tells her mother.
You may want to write about this conflict later, so
keep an eye out for signs of it as you read the
novel.

Through it all, Cora uses her religion, never too
convincingly, to comfort herself. "The Lord can

see into the heart," she says. "If it is His will that some folks has different ideas of honesty from other folks, it is not my place to question His decree."

It's not until halfway through the section that we learn how almost sacrilegious Cora's self-pity is. She rises out of her concerns—petty to the reader, major to her—to take note of Addie for the first time. And you learn that she is sitting by the bedside of a woman whose dying is of less importance to her than her couple of dollars' worth of cakes.

Addie is not far from death. "Her eyes are like two candles when you watch them gutter down into the sockets of iron candle-sticks," Cora says. It's a painful, yet perfectly apt description—the sort of matter-of-fact simile you might expect a country woman to come up with.

Addie has been propped up so that she can look out the window at Cash building her coffin. Cora instinctively links her to her own concerns about the rejected cakes. "They turned out real nice," Cora says. "But not like the cakes Addie used to bake."

Cora's eye falls on the dirty pillow case, giving her a chance to mentally criticize Addie's daughter, who sits by the bed fanning her mother. (In later sections you will learn that the daughter's name is Dewey Dell, and that she is 17 years old.) In the next breath, Cora praises Addie's baking and makes a lame attempt to reassure everyone that "first thing we know [Addie will] be up and baking again." Cora's monologue ends with Darl's entrance into the house.

Take a moment to analyze the way Faulkner creates Cora. He puts the technique of the interior monologue to excellent use here, mixing spoken and unspoken thoughts with sometimes hilarious effect. To see how Faulkner uses this technique, go back over this section and read only those lines that were spoken aloud. The spoken thoughts leave you with no humor at all—just a mother and her daughters exchanging small talk at the bedside of a dying neighbor.

3. DARL

In this section, Faulkner gives you a second glimpse of the workings of Darl's remarkable mind. He exposes you to Jewel's violent nature and his ambivalence toward his horse, the one possession that sets him apart from the other Bundrens.

At the end of Cora's section, Darl walked toward the back of the house. Now, you see where he was heading—to the back porch for a drink from the water bucket.

Vernon Tull, Cora's husband, is sitting there with Anse Bundren, Darl's father. Anse asks, "Where's Jewel?" and Darl, savoring this "warmish-cool" water that he is drinking from a gourd, takes a long time answering.

The water sets off a chain of associations. It brings back memories of hot nights during Darl's childhood and the almost mystical experience of taking a drink, alone, under the starry sky. In one of the many poetic passages in the novel, Darl recalls "a star or two in the bucket, and maybe in the dipper a star or two before I drank."

His thoughts float naturally from the sensual pleasure of the water's taste to an early period of sexual awareness, when he would keep himself awake until the others had gone to sleep. Then "I could lie with my shirt-tail up, . . . feeling myself without touching myself, feeling the cool silence blowing upon my parts. . . ."

NOTE: Sexual Themes in *As I Lay Dying*

Sexuality plays an important role in this book, as in most of Faulkner's works. This theme was alluded to in an early description of Jewel and in Cora's section. It will recur again and again in *As I Lay Dying*—as a source of tension between men and women, as an antidote to loneliness, and as a bid for immortality, by projecting oneself into the future through children and grandchildren. Some readers see sexuality here both as a source of temptation and sin, and as a force for the renewal of life.

Darl finishes drinking and makes an observation about the weather before finally answering Anse. Jewel, he says, is "down to the barn. . . . Harnessing the team."

But he knows that isn't true. A clairvoyant (someone who can see objects or actions removed from natural viewing), Darl can see Jewel "fooling with that horse." Study Darl's description of the violence Jewel inflicts upon the horse—violence that seems to be Jewel's way of expressing love. Darl reports Jewel cutting off the horse's wind supply with one hand and, with the other, stroking its neck. All the while Jewel curses the horse "with obscene ferocity." What kind of person is this?

NOTE: Allusion to Greek Myth The horse is no ordinary animal, and Jewel's relation to it is rather special, too. Faulkner makes sure you know that with two fleeting references to ancient myth. As the horse stands on its hind legs, slashing at

Jewel, "Jewel is enclosed by a glittering maze of hooves as by an illusion of wings. . . ." Suddenly, the horse has become Pegasus, the winged horse of Greek mythology. Pegasus and his rider, Bellerophon, shared many adventures until Bellerophon tried to ride to the throne of the gods atop Mt. Olympus. Zeus, angered, caused Pegasus to throw Bellerophon to the ground. Crippled and blind, the humiliated Bellerophon wandered alone until he died.

In the next paragraph, Jewel mounts the horse and, together, the two become another mythological creature—a centaur. (Centaurs—half men, half horses—were among the lesser gods in Greek myth.) On horseback, Jewel "flows upward in a stooping swirl like the lash of a whip, his body in mid-air shaped to the horse."

These two references are fine examples of Faulkner's use of what the poet T. S. Eliot called "the mythical method." By evoking characters from Greek and biblical myth, Faulkner offers yardsticks against which you can measure his modern characters. In a sense, he is suggesting parallel narratives—stories that serve as backdrops to the one he is telling. Jewel is neither Bellerophon nor a centaur, exactly. Nor is he exactly Dionysus, as is suggested elsewhere in the novel. But you understand him better when you know how much like these mythical characters he is, and how much he and his actions differ from theirs, too.

Will Jewel risk the gods' wrath on his Pegasus? Will he prove to be a savage, coarse centaur? You may want to write a report on his relation to myth, so stay tuned.

4. JEWEL

This brief, passionate section provides the only glimpse you'll get of the way Jewel's mind works. His anger, his hatreds, and his love for his mother clog his consciousness.

One way to get a grip on this section is to tote up the targets of Jewel's anger: (1) Cash enrages him by his "hammering and sawing on that goddamn box." Perhaps jealously, he mocks what he sees as Cash's attempt to win Addie's praise by crafting a coffin outside her window. (2) The Tulls and Dewey Dell, "sitting there, like buzzards" also infuriate Jewel. Even the fanning makes him angry, because it keeps "the air always moving so fast" on Addie's face. (3) People who might pass on the road get him mad, too. Jewel imagines them stopping and praising Cash's carpentry.

What he really wants is to be Addie's lone protector during her last moments of life. In the violent passage that ends the section, Jewel has a fantasy: "It would just be me and her on a high hill and me rolling the rocks down . . . at their faces . . . until she was quiet. . . ."

Despite the violent imagery, this is really a touching section. So far, Jewel offers the only genuine expression of love for Addie that you've seen.

NOTE: Echoes of the Old Testament   The biblical references in *As I Lay Dying* help to explain Faulkner's purpose. Some readers stress the importance of the novel's few Christian images, which appear in later sections.

Other readers find echoes of the "pre-Christian" Old Testament throughout the book—in the cadences of some of the soliloquies, the themes, and some of the characters' attitudes. Indeed, it is possible to find strong overtones of the Book of Job in the novel. God permitted Satan to test Job, "a perfect and upright man" in God's view. Everything Job owns is destroyed, and he is afflicted with sores. Four friends gather round him, ostensibly to comfort him. But their comfort consists of accusations that Job cannot be just, as he claims, and that he must be guilty of arrogant pride.

The parallels here will become obvious as the story unfolds. It's possible to see Addie as Job, and people such as the Tulls, who gather around her ("like buzzards," Jewel says), as Job's quarrelsome friends. The subject of the Book of Job is the problem of good and evil in the world. "Why do the just suffer and the wicked flourish?" the story's prologue asks. Jewel, echoing Job's laments, wonders "if there is a God what the hell is He for." Why, Jewel wonders, doesn't God protect his mother from suffering?

5. DARL

In this key section, Faulkner reveals, in a matter-of-fact way, the promise that propels the entire story forward. At the same time, he pulls back the veil, ever so slightly, on the motivations and foibles of his characters.

NOTE: Faulkner's Use of Pronouns Faulkner's stream of consciousness technique requires him to present pronouns without always clearly establishing their antecedents—the nouns which the pronouns stand for. An instance occurs in the first sentence of this section. This potentially confusing use of pronouns annoys some readers, especially in later sections, when Darl and Vardaman use "it" several times in a row, implying a different— and unspecified—antecedent each time.

In using pronouns this way, Faulkner is working toward verisimilitude—representing thought processes as they actually occur. He is merely trying to reproduce, or at least suggest, the mental shorthand that we all use in our private thoughts.

The comical Anse is played against the serious Anse in this scene, giving you a sense of two sides to his character. Darl wants his father to give the go-ahead to a plan to haul a load of lumber. Anse can't make up his mind. He doesn't want his sons away with the wagon because he has promised Addie he will take her for burial to her hometown, Jefferson, as soon as she dies. "She'll want to start right away," Anse says. "I know her."

This man is generally seen as an object of ridicule. In a circus, he'd be wearing a pair of oversized shoes and patched clothes. Faulkner takes Anse's shoes off, gives him a hunchback, and makes him toothless and unshaven. The way he mangles the language—with a touch of pomposity—only adds to his ridiculousness.

And yet, Faulkner portrays this bumbler with affection. He shows that Anse means well and seems sincere about his intention to respect Addie's wishes. What effect does this have on your assessment of Anse?

Anse never really grants permission for the lumber-hauling trip. Jewel impatiently walks off the porch. Anse sees they are going and tries to recoup a measure of dignity by telling them to be back by sundown the next day.

Why is Darl so eager to make the trip at such a critical point? Some readers, noting the tension between Darl and Jewel, have concluded that Darl has an ulterior motive. If you were told that Darl wants to prevent Jewel from being present at his mother's death, what would your reaction be?

Certainly Jewel seems, to Darl, to have been Addie's favorite. "Ma always whipped him and petted him more," he says, because his height made him stand out. "That's why she named him Jewel," Darl says.

Is Darl's perception of Addie's favoritism accurate? Or is he merely throwing you a false clue? It's hard to tell at this point.

Jewel is certainly true to form. He lashes out at Vernon Tull and accuses everyone of "burning hell" to see Addie dead and buried.

Anse misinterprets Jewel's anger, showing how little he understands about Jewel. "You got no affection nor gentleness for her," he says. "You never had."

What do you learn about Addie here? From Darl, we hear she had a favorite child. From Anse, we hear she is a "private woman" and neat, "ever one to clean up after herself."

Notice how the two brothers make their exits here.

6. CORA

Once more, Cora provides comic relief, this time with a syrupy monologue that suggests she is not attuned to the drama that is unfolding around her. Her monologue would be a marvelous set piece (a section of a work of art strong enough to stand on its own) if you could appreciate its humor without reading earlier sections. But the humor depends on irony—our knowledge that she doesn't know what she's talking about.

The first line—"It was the sweetest thing I ever saw"—sets the tone and lets us know we're in for another string of platitudes. Faulkner delays his punch line in this extended joke, so it's a long while before you learn what she sees. By that time, her credibility as a reporter has been so destroyed, you end up wondering if she saw anything at all.

Somehow, Cora has persuaded herself that Darl has gone to haul a load of lumber against his will. "But nothing would do but Anse and Jewel must make that three dollars," Cora says.

What does this misinterpretation allow her to do? Cora wouldn't have expected anything better from Anse, she says. But she is outraged that the lure of three dollars would induce Jewel to turn his back on the mother who showed him "downright partiality."

She exempts Darl from her blanket condemnation. On his way out of the house, he stopped by Addie's door. "He just stood and looked at his dying mother, his heart too full for words."

Dewey Dell gives another version of the same scene in the next section. In its own way, as you will see, her version is as complicated as Cora's. By putting two opposite interpretations of the same event side by side, Faulkner is calling attention to the subjective nature of experience. The human ability to interpret events in an entirely personal way ensures that there will always be an unbridgeable gap between even close relatives. The isolation of individuals within a group—a seeming paradox—is one of the major themes of *As I Lay Dying*.

7. DEWEY DELL

Dewey Dell is one of Faulkner's most successful comic characters, and in this section you see why. Her name suggests a sensual being, a part of nature. Although Faulkner mocks her, he treats her with affection, as he does Anse.

Half of her brief section is a hilarious attempt to shed the blame for her seduction and subsequent pregnancy. The seducer is someone named Lafe, who has come to help the Bundrens harvest their cotton crop. Woods border the cotton field, and Dewey Dell and Lafe happen to be picking down a row towards this "secret shade."

As they move closer to the trees and Dewey Dell's fever rises, she creates a game that allows her to think that she has no responsibility for her actions. If her sack is full of cotton by the time they reach the woods, she will let herself be seduced. If it isn't full, she will continue picking cotton up the next row, away from the woods.

She may have been thinking out loud. For Lafe ends up picking into her sack. At the end of the row, her sack is full of cotton—"and I could not help it," she says.

NOTE: The Persephone Myth   In Greek myth, there's a lovely story about Persephone, the daughter of Zeus and Demeter. Persephone was the goddess of spring and therefore of fertility. One day Pluto, king of the underworld, or Hades, seized her and held her captive. Her mother, Demeter, as goddess of vegetation the major fertility goddess, managed to persuade the gods to have Persephone returned to her. But Pluto tricked Persephone into eating a pomegranate, the food of the dead. So for four months every year she had to return to the underworld. The flowers and grain died whenever she left the earth, but when she returned, the flowers blossomed and everything grew again. The story symbolizes the annual vegetation cycle—the end of the growing season in the fall and its return in the spring.

Some readers hear echoes of this myth in *As I Lay Dying*. They see the fertile Dewey Dell suggesting Persephone. Lafe, who has come from town to harvest cotton, suggests Pluto. Lafe lured Dewey Dell into the "secret shade," a place whose very name hints at the underworld.

You may want to ponder what all this might mean—if anything. Some readers feel that if Faulkner is using the Persephone myth, he is doing so only to show how far Dewey Dell veers from it. For Dewey Dell is surely not comfortable with her fertility. She will spend a lot of the book thinking about, or actually seeking, an abortion.

Darl has a special relationship with Dewey Dell. They can communicate without speaking. Darl knows she is pregnant, and Dewey Dell hates him for knowing.

At Addie's door—the same door where Cora saw him standing silently—he tells Dewey Dell that Addie is going to die before he and Jewel return. "Then why are you taking Jewel?" she asks. Because, he answers, he wants Jewel to help him load the wagon.

This is all very strange, this conversation without sound. But don't forget that Darl has seemed clairvoyant before, and that, as Cora reported, he's the Bundren "that folks say is queer."

Dewey Dell makes some interesting comments about other family members here. She reinforces the view that Anse is lazy and crafty. And she says that Jewel has concerns that the rest of the family don't share. Her choice of words (he is not "carekin") suggests, in fact, that Jewel is in some way unrelated to the rest of the Bundrens. This is an interesting clue to his character.

8. TULL

Faulkner continues to introduce his cast of characters with this section, narrated by Cora's husband, Vernon. And he brings one of the novel's central images, a fish, into the story for the first time.

Anse and Vernon sit on the back porch after Jewel and Darl have left. Vernon's thoughts wander from the weather ("It's fixing to rain tonight") to the hard life all women have. The men make a reference to the Book of Job. "The Lord giveth," Anse says, reciting part of the prayer in which Job acknowledges and accepts God's will.

Addie's youngest son, Vardaman, comes up the hill carrying a fish he wants to show Addie. It's unclear how old Vardaman is. But if the fish he caught is "nigh as long as he is," it's a fair bet that he isn't older than eight or nine. On Anse's orders, Vardaman lugs the fish away to clean it.

NOTE: Vardaman's Name   Vardaman is named after James Kimble Vardaman (1861–1930), a Mississippi politician who died the year Faulkner wrote *As I Lay Dying*. Vardaman won the governorship in 1903 by exploiting the racial prejudices of poor white farmers like the Bundrens. Faulkner once pointed out that poor whites in Mississippi often named their children after politicians like Vardaman, who pretended to show an interest in their concerns.

At five o'clock, the Tulls say their goodbyes to Anse. Vernon offers to help him bring in his corn. Cash is still working on the coffin outside the house. As they pass him, Vernon mutters a silent hope that Cash will work as carefully on the Tulls' barn as he does on the coffin. As you'll see, nearly everyone in this book has something else besides Addie on their minds.

Vernon Tull seems to be a narrator you can trust, one who passes no judgment on events or people he reports on. Like Dewey Dell and Darl, he points out how dependent on others Anse is. These observations belie Anse's own claim, in section 5, that he has never been "beholden" to anyone.

Even Kate Tull, who continues to smolder over the rejected cakes, notes how dependent Anse is. If Addie dies, she predicts, he'll get another wife "before cotton-picking."

9. ANSE

In this section you learn that the image most people have of Anse is accurate. He's selfish and luckless, and too adept at rationalizing his laziness to make any effort to change his fortunes. Yet Faulkner paints a picture of him that draws our sympathy. Watch how he does it.

Anse stands in front of the house, gazing at the road and contemplating his bad luck. He traces his misfortunes to the road, which brings "every bad luck" to his house.

NOTE: The Image of the Road   Faulkner once told a critic that the idea for *As I Lay Dying* grew out of a story someone told him about a man who was angry at a road because it brought trouble to his house. Preposterous as it seems, Faulkner has Anse develop that idea here.

The passage foreshadows the novel's basic story line. Spectacular calamities will happen on the road to Jefferson.

Significantly, Anse implies that traveling is a flaunting of God's will. God built man to stay put, like a tree, he says. Could he be suggesting that the Bundrens' journey will be in some way a defiance of the gods?

Old Doc Peabody pops into Anse's thoughts without warning. Clues in other sections suggest that Anse sent for him, even though he shudders at the thought of paying a doctor. So it's unclear why he tells Peabody, "I never sent for you." Perhaps that is Anse's way of gaining Peabody's promise not to tell Addie that he had done so.

Peabody goes in to see Addie, leaving Anse to curse his bad luck. He can envision rain coming up the road and finding only his house. In an echo from Job, he wonders why a sinless man must suffer such torment.

Vardaman reappears, bloody from gutting his fish. Anse tells him to wash his hands. The order probably reminds him of Addie, for he thinks of how hard she worked to make her sons "right." Suddenly he feels drained, unable "to get no heart into anything." Vardaman drives Anse's pain home with a question about Addie's health.

As the section ends, Anse isn't crying. Nonetheless, he may remind you of that classic portrait of a clown with a smile painted on his face and a tear rolling down his cheek.

10. DARL

Darl shows an unattractive side to his personality in this short section. He gets a perverse pleasure from taunting Jewel about Addie's death and Dewey Dell about her pregnancy.

Sitting behind Jewel on the wagon, Darl asks his brother again and again if he knows Addie is going to die. Jewel never responds.

Darl then recalls taunting Dewey Dell about her eagerness to get to town. But she can't bring herself to admit that she is pregnant any more than Jewel, in an earlier scene, could refer to his mother's coffin.

Why should Dewey Dell want to get to town? You've probably guessed by now that she hopes to have an abortion.

Faulkner ends the section with an image of Hades, or the underworld. An hour before darkness, the sun "is poised like a bloody egg upon a crest of thunderheads," and the air smells like sulfur. All-knowing, Darl realizes that Peabody will have to be pulled up the steep hill to the Bundrens' house on a rope—"balloon-like up the sulphurous air."

11. PEABODY

In Doc Peabody, you meet one of the most trustworthy outside observers of the Bundren family. A hefty old man, he is full of knowledge and wisdom.

Peabody realized as soon as the weather turned bad that it had been Anse and no one else who called for him. "Nobody but a luckless man could ever need a doctor in the face of a cyclone." He also realized that if Anse thought he needed a doctor, the patient was beyond hope.

NOTE: Death as a State of Mind   Peabody presents his view of death as "merely a function of the mind—and that of the minds of the ones who suffer the bereavement." He disputes those who say death is the end as well as those who call it a beginning. To Peabody, death is just like someone moving out of town and living on in the memory of his former neighbors.

Addie is not yet dead. But you can be sure that, even in death, she will be present in the lives of the survivors. The promise she extracted from Anse—to bury her in Jefferson—will ensure it. The ability of the dead to shape life, to motivate the living, is one of the major themes of the novel.

Outside on the porch, Peabody chews out Anse for waiting so long to call him. Peabody suspects he didn't want to pay a doctor's bill. But Anse suggests—here as in the fifth section—another reason for delaying: his fear that, once Addie saw Peabody, she would simply die.

And that seems to be what has happened. Dewey Dell calls Anse to Addie's bedside. Addie is near death.

Her eyes drive Peabody out of the room. Outside, he can hear Addie call Cash in a strong voice.

Peabody tries to explain why a woman would reject sympathy and help and cling, instead, to Anse, a "trifling animal." Such, Peabody says, is "the love that passeth understanding: that pride, that furious desire to hide that abject nakedness which we bring here with us [and] carry . . . with us into the earth again."

We are back to Job again: "Naked I came out of my mother's womb," Job said, "and naked shall I return." We are born alone and we die alone, Peabody seems to say, but we spend our days trying to deny it.

NOTE: The Bundrens' Pride In order to understand what motivates the Bundrens—especially Addie—it's important to understand their pride. In general, pride is a lofty, sometimes arrogant, sense of one's own superiority. To many Christians, pride is a sin—an attempt to set oneself up as better than God. Elihu, one of Job's four counselors, accuses him of provoking God's wrath with his arrogant pride. (Cora will accuse Addie of such sinful behavior in section 39.)

In Faulkner's view, however, pride needn't be a negative value. He sees it as essential to man's dignity. It can and does, in this book, mean strength—the dignity that can hold a family together and enable it to overcome adversity. In a sense, the Bundrens' pride is of this heroic sort, as their journey to Jefferson will show.

12. DARL

Darl, with his clairvoyance, details the scene of Addie's death even though he is miles away at the time.

Addie's death is a special moment, one full of clues to many of the characters. Anse, Vardaman, and Dewey Dell are in the room when she dies.

Anse, ill at ease, is clumsy and touching by turns. While trying to tell her where Darl and Jewel are, he breaks off as if he doubts his own explanation. He puts his hand on hers just as she sits up to look out the window and call Cash. She dies looking at Vardaman, who backs out of the room in horror.

Cash comes to the room. Anse's sense of timing is off, as always. He queries Cash about his progress on the coffin while Cash is trying to come to grips with his loss. Without looking at Anse, Cash goes back to work. Anse tells Dewey to get some supper ready. She leaves, and Anse is alone with Addie. He touches her face and her hands and makes some awkward attempts to smooth the quilt covering her. He gives up and breaks the solemnity of the scene with the words, "God's will be done. Now I can get them teeth."

Three italicized paragraphs break up Darl's description of Addie's death. In one of them, Faulkner has Darl explain his and Jewel's plight. At the moment of their mother's death, they are stuck in a rainy ditch with a broken wheel.

In the second italicized paragraph, Darl reports an inconclusive exchange between Peabody and Dewey Dell. Peabody tries to comfort her. She tries to tell him how he could help her with an abortion. Yet, still unable to say the word "pregnant," even to herself, she cannot make her need clear.

The third italicized paragraph ends this section with Darl's announcement to Jewel that Addie is dead. Darl reports no reaction from Jewel, who at the time is straining against the axle, trying to raise it.

It's curious how quickly Anse and Dewey Dell lapse into their own private concerns as soon as Addie is dead. Cash returns to his work, Jewel and Darl to theirs. Only Vardaman seems overwhelmed with grief.

13. VARDAMAN

In psychiatry, a trauma is a startling experience that has lasting effect on someone's mind. With this monologue, Faulkner gives you an "inside look" at a young boy's reaction to a traumatic event—his mother's death.

In the previous section, Vardaman was backing out of the room where his mother died. Now he has run through the house to the rear porch. Crying, he realizes he is standing near the spot where he dropped the fish when he first brought it home. He realizes that the fish is dead—"not-fish"—like his mother, who "is getting so far ahead I cannot catch her."

In the next paragraph, thoughts of his mother and the fish occur side by side, too. Thinking by analogy, he realizes that he killed and cut up the fish and assumes that someone must have killed his mother. Since she died after Peabody came, he blames Peabody. He rushes to the barn to get a stick, possibly intending to hit Peabody.

NOTE: Jewel's Horse Pause to examine how Faulkner treats Jewel's horse in this section. Inside the barn, Vardaman leans against its warm body and cries, the way a child in pain might seek his mother's warmth. Like a mother, the horse is a life-giving force, and it seems to give Vardaman strength. "The life in him runs under the skin. . . . I can smell the life running up from under my hands, up my arms, and then I can leave the stall." Later, Darl will taunt Jewel about his mother being a horse, and you may want to return to this paragraph to piece together his meaning.

Vardaman doesn't hit Peabody. Instead, he strikes Peabody's horses, who race off pulling the buggy.

Back in the barn, Faulkner throws in a little comic relief in the segment about the lowing cow. Dewey Dell calls Vardaman for dinner. His mind returns to the fish that was alive one minute and dead the next. He can't make sense of it—of death. "And now she's gittin ready to cook hit."

14. DEWEY DELL

This section shows you Dewey Dell trying to cope with the burdens of her pregnancy and the chores she inherited from her mother. It also gives you a closer look at a mind unable to follow any train of thought for long.

Dewey Dell's monologue begins where Darl's

report on her in section 12 left off. She is thinking that Peabody could help her end her pregnancy. She leaps from one idea to another and ends in frustration, because Peabody doesn't know she's pregnant and she can't tell him.

NOTE: Dewey Dell's Isolation   One thread of thought is worth tracing here, because Dewey Dell touches on the theme of isolation that Faulkner pursues throughout the novel. In the second paragraph, she says that if she could feel the baby's presence she would not be alone.

Try to "translate" the rest of the paragraph. She seems to contradict herself twice. She says she would not be alone if she had an abortion, and that "Then I could be all right alone."

It sounds like gibberish, and many readers believe it *is* gibberish. Others, however, see no contradictions at all. She wouldn't be alone if she had an abortion, they explain, because Peabody would have her secret in his mind. But in another sense, she would be alone. She would not be carrying a child.

Her actions are as random as her mental processes. She stashes the mutilated fish in the cupboard, puts turnip greens and buttermilk on the table, and leaves the house to milk the cow and stare at the pine clumps where she was seduced. While she is doing all this, her thoughts jump about, from what Peabody could do for her, to Lafe and "the process of coming unalone"—of uniting with Lafe.

She finds Vardaman in the barn. He is relieved

to see that Dewey Dell shares his anger about Peabody.

After Vardaman leaves, she gazes at the "secret
clumps." She sees lightning in the distance. Everything else is "dead": the oppressive air, the earth,
the darkness. In the last line, Faulkner reminds
you that amid these images of death Dewey Dell
is, like Persephone, a life-giving, fertile part of nature—"like a wet seed wild in the hot blind earth."

15. VARDAMAN

Vardaman continues to grope for an understanding of his mother's death. Study the way
Faulkner captures a child's mind by showing it
rather than describing it.

Pausing over the first paragraph here, as in the
other sections, will help you get your bearings.
Vardaman is watching Cash finish the coffin, and
he is thinking of the time he got shut up in a corn
crib. He remembers how hard it was to breathe,
and he remembers his fear.

NOTE: Faulkner's Use of Objective Correlatives
If someone tells you about a beautiful, smiling baby,
how do you feel? The description might make people who love babies feel happy. For them, the baby
objectifies happiness.

The U.S.-born British poet T. S. Eliot (1888–1965)
mastered the art of presenting emotions as objects,
or even scenes, and having his readers "feel" what
he was talking about. He called these scenes, or
objects, "objective correlatives." Faulkner, a great
fan of Eliot, uses objective correlatives throughout
As I Lay Dying to get you to experience his characters' feelings.

What feeling is he trying to have you share in the opening paragraph of this section? What words does he use? How does he use punctuation to heighten this feeling?

Vardaman associates being shut up in a corn crib with being shut up in a coffin. It's not a very apt analogy, because Addie is dead. But Vardaman, in real pain ("the bleeding plank" is the clue here, if any is needed), has taken the adults at their word (see section 12) and decided that Addie has literally gone away. The trouble is, he can't find her, or "catch her," as he said in section 13.

He's convinced now that the woman lying in the bed was not his mother. "She went away when the other one laid down on her bed. . . ."

Since he knows he couldn't breathe in the corn crib, he knows his mother—he is sure she is still alive—couldn't breathe in a nailed-up coffin. And so he's sure she wouldn't allow herself to be nailed up. "So if she lets him it is not her." Only an impostor would let Cash nail her into a coffin.

But if the dead woman is an impostor, where is Addie? The fish he caught and cut up pops into his mind. Before the fish showed up, his mother was alive. "Then it wasn't and she was, and now it is and she wasn't."

He decides, without saying it yet, that his mother *is* the fish. Tomorrow the family will eat it. "And she will be him and pa and Cash and Dewey Dell. . . ."

The imagined eating of the fish serves as a Christian reference, some readers believe. In this view, the chopped-up fish is a parallel to the symbolic eating and drinking of Christ in Holy Communion as a way of preventing the believer's death. You will have a chance to further explore this interpretation in the discussion of section 19.

As this section ends, Vardaman remembers that Vernon Tull saw the fish. Maybe he can find it, he figures, if he gets Vernon to help him.

NOTE: Bananas and Electric Trains Something else you learned in this section is that Dewey Dell whetted Vardaman's appetite for the journey to Jefferson. Apparently she promised that they'll get bananas there—a real luxury for a poor country boy—and maybe look at an electric train in a store window. Now Vardaman has a goal in Jefferson, just like Anse and Dewey Dell.

---

16. TULL

In this section, you see the first stirrings among the Bundrens' neighbors as they hear of Addie's death.

Cora takes the arrival of Peabody's panicked team of horses as a sign that Addie is dead. But Vernon is in no mind to hitch the team and drive to the Bundrens'. He wants to sleep.

Vardaman wakes the Tulls around midnight. He has walked four miles through the mud to get there, and all he wants to talk about is the fish. "He's outen his head with grief and worry," Cora says, quite sensibly. Vernon thinks she may be going a bit far to say that Vardaman's confusion is God's judgment on Anse Bundren. "The Lord's got more to do than that. He's bound to have. Because the only burden Anse Bundren's ever had is himself."

NOTE: Folk Humor in Faulkner America has a strong tradition of homespun, or folk, humor. Most humorists in this tradition lace their stories with seemingly naïve comments that on closer inspection often turn out to be nuggets of wisdom. It is this irony—the tension between what a person seems to say and what he is actually saying—that triggers the laughs.

Faulkner makes Vernon Tull one of the art's most engaging practitioners. It's hard to believe that Tull could answer the door, hold up his lamp, and miss seeing Vardaman, no matter how short the boy is. He's spinning a tall tale—something you know is preposterous, but which you allow the teller to get away with because it's so entertaining.

There are many instances of folk humor in this section alone. The matter-of-fact way Tull tells how Addie got two holes bored into her face is a fine example of the grotesque violence that occurs in many tall tales. How did you react to this scene? With shock? Laughter? Both?

With Vardaman sitting between them, Cora and Vernon drive through the rain to the Bundrens'. There, Vernon helps Cash finish the coffin.

Vardaman opens the windows next to Addie's bed twice, to let her breathe. This prepares you for his boring holes through the coffin lid later.

17. DARL

Of all the Bundrens, Darl so far seems the most perceptive and reflective. He alone is clairvoyant, as has been shown earlier. Faulkner calls attention to these powers in this section, where Darl describes still another scene that he does not witness in person.

Faulkner handles the opening in an almost cinematic way. He focuses our attention first on the source of light—a sooty, cracked lantern—and then on the scene its "feeble and sultry glare" illuminates. Cash continues to labor over the coffin. The saw's shadow is about six feet long and appears to be cutting through Anse's "shabby and aimless silhouette."

NOTE: The Scent of Sulfur The air still smells of sulfur. As pointed out earlier, that could be a tipoff that in Faulkner's view the Bundrens inhabit some sort of underworld. Sulfur is the brimstone, or burning stone, associated with Hell and the fiery punishments inflicted there.

Anse is no help at all. Cash sends him into the house to "get something to cover the lantern" from the rain. Anse returns from his mission wearing Jewel's raincoat and carrying Dewey Dell's, which Cash uses to make a roof over the lantern. It wouldn't occur to Anse to offer the raincoat he's wearing to his son.

The Tulls arrive and lend Cora's raincoat to Cash. Vernon helps Cash finish the coffin. Anse keeps himself busy picking up tools and laying them down. After Anse accidentally knocks down the makeshift roof over the lantern, Cash ushers him into the house to keep him out of trouble.

NOTE: The Depth of Anse's Grief Anse is such a complicated character, and Faulkner handles him so ambiguously, that it's hard to tell how he feels about Addie's death. Perhaps he's not even sure himself. In the rain, his own face is twice shown to be "streaming," as if with tears.

Faulkner describes his wet face as "a monstrous burlesque of all bereavement"—a mockery, not the real thing at all. In section 14, there also seemed something phony about his momentary inability to eat. Some readers think he is too selfish and too emotionally dead to mourn. Others think he just does not know how, although he feels a duty to do so. Still others feel he is genuinely grieved by his loss but too much of a bumbler to show it plainly.

There's a fine passage toward the end of the section that lets you see how Faulkner can shift moods unexpectedly, sometimes with comic effect. It has stopped raining. In the dark before dawn, the men carry the completed coffin into the house and place it next to Addie's bed. Faulkner captures the solemnity of the moment by describing their slow, careful, awkward movements "as though for a long time they have not walked on floors." Then Peabody says, "Let's eat a snack," and the solemnity evaporates as abruptly as it did in section 12 when Anse said, "Now I can get them teeth."

In both cases, Faulkner brings you back suddenly to the petty concerns of the living. Can you suggest why?

In the final two paragraphs, you are with Darl's thoughts as he and Jewel lie awake in a "strange room" miles away. He is questioning himself, wondering not just who he is but whether he exists at all.

This is the first sign you get that Darl may be

haunted by such questions. Maybe Vernon Tull was on to something when he said that Darl's main problem is thinking too much.

18. CASH

Faulkner presents Cash's thought processes here in an unusual way—in the form of a list. The subject of the list is structure—of houses, beds, bodies, and coffins. But the list also mimics the structure of Cash's mind.

A list is an arresting format and, in Cash's case, it seems an appropriate one. Cash is a methodical man, as you have seen already. He took infinite care on the coffin, planing off the inside edges of its lid and sides.

This beveling to make the lid fit snugly was time-consuming, as Tull pointed out. But Cash has his reasons for spending the extra time, and he presents them here.

As you read them, you may dismiss some as nonsensical. To an educated mind, it may seem ignorant to speak of the "sideways" stress on a bed's joints and of the "slanting" stress caused by a dead body's animal magnetism. But Cash is simply piecing together elements of folk wisdom into a coherent set of principles to guide his work. The methodical nature of the list reflects his methodical mind.

The 13th and final entry—"It makes a neater job"—may seem to you the most important reason for beveling the coffin's lid and sides. Not to Cash. Can you think why?

19. VARDAMAN

This is the shortest of the 59 sections, yet it has raised, to many readers, several knotty problems.

What is Vardaman getting at by equating his mother with a fish? Is there a larger symbolic meaning here that provides a key to understand *As I Lay Dying*? This is a good place to pause and make a stab at those questions.

NOTE: Vardaman's Mental Faculties   Some readers have assumed that Vardaman is retarded, like the character Benjy Compson in Faulkner's *The Sound and the Fury*. Other readers feel that he seems irrational only after Addie dies and he tries to make sense of the mystery of her death. The trauma of his mother's death and his primitive idea of the world lead him to a conclusion that seems entirely logical to his young and troubled mind. This view got support from Faulkner himself, who told a college class in the 1950s that Vardaman is not retarded.

---

20. TULL

Addie's funeral takes place the morning after her death. Vernon Tull describes the day from the time he returned to the Bundrens' at ten o'clock in the morning until he took his family home again in the wagon. In the interval you meet some neighbors, get a glimpse of Preacher Whitfield.

You learn in the first paragraph that the river has been rising to record heights and that the bridge across it is in danger of collapsing. Whitfield shows up with the news that it has fallen. Lon Quick II, the son of the man who sold Jewel the horse, notes that God will probably help Anse get Addie across the river somehow. "He's took care of Anse a long time, now," he says. Another man chimes in, echoing Tull's thought in section 8: "I reckon He's like everybody else around here. He's done it so long now He cant quit."

NOTE: Sense of Community   This remark is a reminder that the Bundrens and their poor white neighbors are part of a community. They are much like a family, looking out for one another, even for ne'er-do-wells like Anse. There's a sense of solidarity about them that's reflected in the way they extend helping hands to the Bundrens. The paradox—and a major theme—of the novel, however, is that none of these people can ever really communicate with each other, no matter how closely their lives are intertwined.

Watch Anse in this section. He is like a man transformed. Tull twice notes his dignity. How can you account for it?

Note Whitfield, too. You'll get a closer look at him in section 41, where you may have to revise the opinion of him you pick up here. Tull points out that his voice doesn't seem to belong with his body. The voice is "triumphant and sad"; the body, mud splattered, smaller than the voice.

On the way home, the Tulls pass Vardaman, who is fishing in a swampy pool. Do you suppose he's hoping to find his mother returned to life?

This section has some grotesque humor. They lay Addie backwards in the coffin to avoid wrinkling the flared skirt of her wedding dress. Then the women fashion a veil out of mosquito netting to hide the auger holes in her face.

Another bit of humor mocks Cash's precise mind.

He describes his fall from a church roof as "Twenty-eight foot, four and a half inches, about."

NOTE: Italicized Sections   Faulkner isolates two segments in italics here. The first segment contains assorted banter that Tull hears as he talks with Cash. The second section is a flash-forward. Faulkner uses it to tell you that it was three days before Darl and Jewel got the wagon fixed and loaded Addie onto it. That's a long time to keep a body above ground in July heat.

---

21. DARL

This is the first of three short sections that conclude the first part of the novel. Here, you see Darl taunt Jewel as the two approach their home three days after Addie's death.

Darl points out the buzzards that hang in the sky high above the house. They both know why the buzzards are there. Yet it seems Darl can't resist infuriating Jewel by saying, "But it's not your horse that's dead."

Jewel's mind is riveted on the horse he cannot see, shaping it in his mind. When they reach the barn, Jewel enters his horse's stall and pulls himself into the loft. His only sound has been an angry curse at Darl.

NOTE: Jewel's Mother as a Horse   What does Darl mean when he says that Jewel's mother is a horse? Here are three interpretations you might consider:

1. With Addie dead, Darl has nothing he can love with the intensity that one might love a mother. Jewel does. He has a horse. Thus, Darl reasons, Jewel's mother is a horse.

2. Jewel yearned for an exclusive relationship with his mother—the sort he described in his monologue early in the book. Yet he couldn't have such a relationship, so he bought a substitute. The horse is his own possession, something so wild that no one else can approach it.

3. In Greek mythology, both Demeter, goddess of fertility and harvests, and Dionysus, god of fertility and wine, are associated with the horse. Dionysus, in fact, was also a god of the trees. Readers who see the "wooden" Jewel as a kind of Dionysus see the horse as his "fructifying [fruit-bearing] spirit"—the fertilizing spirit that enables him to be virile. Faulkner was familiar with James G. Frazer's 1890 study of mythology, *The Golden Bough*, which called the horse "the fructifying spirit both of the tree and of the Corn." Demeter, goddess of harvests, was also known as the Corn-Spirit. The horse is thus Jewel's link to Addie, who many readers see as a sort of Demeter.

---

22. CASH

Cash was obsessed with building the proper "balance" into the coffin. Now he hopes to maintain that balance in transit. It seems he wants Darl and Jewel to carry Addie's coffin to the wagon in a way that will allow the coffin to "tote and ride on a balance." But Jewel, able to act only impulsively, orders his brothers to "Pick up!"

23. DARL

Darl describes the scene begun in section 22. Jewel
rushes ahead with the coffin, leaving Cash limping
behind. Jewel thrusts it onto the wagon. In "fury
and despair," he curses Darl as the section ends.

24. VARDAMAN

Except for Jewel, who is heading to the barn,
everyone is on the way to the wagon or in it. Anse
orders Jewel to leave the horse home, but Jewel
doesn't stop. "Jewel's mother is a horse," Darl says.

Vardaman still has it in his own mind that his
mother is a fish. So Darl's comment sets off a
charming discussion about their mother's and their
own existence.

Anse is making a vain attempt to take charge.
He doesn't like the idea that Cash is bringing his
toolbox along, that Jewel wants to take his horse,
and that Dewey Dell carries a package that she
says contains Cora Tull's cakes. "It ain't right,"
Anse says. "It's a flouting of the dead."

All the while, Anse is no doubt thinking of the
false teeth he wants. Vardaman has a hard time
getting his mind off the electric trains he hopes to
see.

Many novelists want their readers to relate to
the situations they present. How is it possible for
us to make connections with such far-out situations?

25. DARL

Darl gives another view of what Vardaman reported in the earlier section. He studies Jewel, who
is approaching the barn, and then he shifts his

attention to Dewey Dell. Peabody is there; Darl can see his reflection in Dewey Dell's eyes.

The wagon moves, and as it does the buzzards disappear. Anse thinks he has convinced Jewel to leave his horse home.

NOTE: Description of Dewey Dell Darl describes Dewey Dell's leg in a way that may reveal more about Faulkner's view of her. Darl speaks of "that lever which moves the world; one of that caliper which measures the length and breadth of life." What do you think Faulkner is saying about women with these two metaphors, one of a lever and the other of a caliper (an instrument that measures diameters)? Is he identifying her as a life force, someone literally capable of moving the world? How could her two legs, spreading and closing like a caliper, take the measure of life?

---

26. ANSE

Anse bemoans his luck throughout the monologue. He feels that Jewel is showing disrespect for his mother by bringing the horse. And he feels Darl is showing disrespect, too, sitting on the plank seat above his mother, laughing. Clearly there is something odd about Darl. Cora called him "queer," and now Anse says that his behavior has made him a figure of gossip.

The laughter appears to have been triggered by Jewel's appearance on horseback. What could be so funny about that? Perhaps Darl is laughing at his father's impotent anger. Maybe, as some readers have suggested, he is laughing at the absurdity of the whole scene.

Through Anse's eyes, the Darl who sits laughing on the wagon seems to be a personality in the process of disintegration. Scour the next section for clues that might persuade you to accept or reject this view.

27. DARL

In this section, you get Darl's description of Jewel's arrival on horseback. As the Bundrens pass Tull's place four miles from home, the wagon maintains a "dreamlike" pace. In contrast, Jewel is all motion, "the horse driving, its hooves hissing in the mud."

Cash realizes that the body is decaying and says that "in a couple of days now it'll be smelling." Darl bares his hostility toward Jewel with his response. He suggests that Cash share his thoughts about decay with Jewel. When Cash worries about the coffin's "balance," Darl suggests he tell that to Jewel, too.

As Jewel's horse passes the wagon its hoof splatters a "gout of mud" onto the coffin. Patiently, as he does everything, Cash wipes away this insult with a leaf.

NOTE: Darl's Elevated Language   Some readers have criticized the book on the grounds that Darl doesn't sound like an uneducated hill farmer in his monologues. "We go on," he says in this section, "with a motion so soporific, so dreamlike as to be uninferant of progress, as though time and not space were decreasing between us and it."

When he speaks aloud, however, he sounds more like a creature of his environment. "I haven't got ere one," he says in section 24. To many readers, the disparity between the way he speaks and the way he thinks is perfectly acceptable. To others, the elevated, poetic style of his thoughts makes him somewhat unbelievable.

28. ANSE

In this brief section, Anse sums up his view of life, of the hard times that "the hardworking man, the farmer" has to endure. He appears to put himself in that category—a piece of comic irony that may make you laugh.

The family makes it to the Samsons' house at "dusk-dark" and learns that the bridge they had hoped to cross has been washed out. Somewhat like Cora, Anse shrouds himself in the Scriptures for solace and protection. But what truly revives his enthusiasm is the thought that "now I can get them teeth. That will be a comfort. It will." Since this book is filled with symbolism, what could Anse's teeth stand for, in your opinion?

29. SAMSON

Samson is one of eight characters whose interior monologues Faulkner produces to give you "outsiders' views" of the Bundrens. Thus, this section gives you something to measure the Bundrens' perceptions against.

The men sitting on Samson's porch around sundown are surprised to see the Bundrens come into view. They don't realize at first that the wagon is carrying Addie's coffin. The younger Lon Quick goes down to the road to tell them that the bridge is out. He returns to the house leading the wagon, his face looking "funny, around the nostrils."

Samson invites the Bundrens to stay for the night. He tries to persuade Anse to take Addie back to New Hope in the morning and bury her there. Apparently he nearly succeeds, because when he returns to the barn, he discovers Dewey Dell insisting that Anse take the body to Jefferson. "If you dont do it, it will be a curse on you," she tells Anse.

NOTE: Dramatic Irony   Samson doesn't understand the real reason behind Dewey Dell's insistence. From earlier clues, you are well aware of her reasons. This episode offers one of the novel's many instances of dramatic irony (when the audience understands the implications or meaning of an action or statement, and the characters do not).

Dewey Dell's argument works. Anse refuses to hear any more talk from Samson about burying Addie in New Hope.

NOTE: The Samsons' Neighborliness   The values that bind the Bundrens and their neighbors into a community are very much evident in this chapter. Like the Tulls, the Samsons look after the Bundrens, even though they don't think highly of them. The Samsons' sense of obligation to their neighbors is so great that Samson considers the Bundrens' refusal to accept his wife Rachel's food as an insult.

And yet, despite all this concern and sense of

community, Faulkner makes clear in a number of ways that the Samsons understand the Bundrens no more than the Bundrens understand each other. The two families' sleeping arrangements symbolize the gap between them. This is one more example of the book's theme that even people who are united in a common purpose live in isolation from one another.

At the end, you don't know what the Bundrens' plans are. Samson just hears them drive off toward New Hope. He supposes they can cross the river "up by Mount Vernon," which would put them 18 miles from Jefferson.

30. DEWEY DELL

Dewey Dell's confused thoughts reach a fever pitch in this section. Her mixed feelings about her abortion and her mother's death clash with the memory of a nightmare and a homicidal fantasy about Darl. Faulkner sets some of her deeper and more urgent reflections in italics.

As the sign indicating the turn for New Hope looms into sight, Dewey Dell reaches a moment of decision. Should she tell Anse to turn? If she does, she realizes, *"We wont have to go to town."* Notice she doesn't say, "We wont *be able* to go to town." Why do you suppose she doesn't?

Look for answers to that question in the flurry of thoughts—many of them incomplete—that surround her statement. She thinks of the "agony and the despair of spreading bones"—a birth image, perhaps, similar to the feeling she had in section 14.

This thought runs into a description of Darl focusing his eyes on her. As his eyes rise to her face, she feels them strip her naked, exposing her. Abruptly she recalls a nightmare of waking "with a black void rushing under me" and of Vardaman stabbing a fish. She thinks of killing Darl. This series of images—an objective correlative that evokes hate—is her fiercest thought yet in association with Darl.

Her thought of murder butts against her memory of the nightmare she began to think about in the previous paragraph. You don't have to understand this nightmare to realize what it reveals about Dewey Dell's emotions. It is another objective correlative—a story that calls up the emotion Faulkner wants you to share with Dewey Dell. Is the emotion fear? Terror? Whatever it is, the emotion provides the context for her fleeting thought about not having to go to Jefferson. She is frightened and for a moment unsure that she wants an abortion.

NOTE: "I believe in God"   They pass the turn off to New Hope, and Dewey Dell expresses her faith in God. Why do you suppose she does this, here and at the end of the chapter, after reporting Darl's taunt to Jewel about the buzzard? Have you ever decided on a course of action without knowing where it would lead? If so, you might have said something like, "Well, now it's in the hands of fate."

Dewey Dell contrived to put herself in the hands of fate during her seduction by Lafe. She seems to be doing something of the same sort here.

---

31. TULL

The fact that the Bundren family is a study in contrasts is never made clearer than in this section. Read this section to learn how the Bundrens' many differences shape their reactions to obstacles.

Tull has hitched his mule to his wagon and followed the Bundrens to the banks of the swollen river. They're sitting in their wagon looking at the collapsed bridge when he catches up to them.

NOTE: Anse's Reaction to the Bridge Tull can't fathom Anse's attitude. He finds the head of the Bundren clan looking at the bridge with a "kind of pleased astonishment." Samson, in section 29, noticed Anse react in a similar way when he heard how high the water had risen. "I be durn," Samson said, "if he didn't act like he was proud of it, like he had made the river rise himself." What could Faulkner be getting at, describing Anse this way? Could it be that Anse *is* pleased, secretly glad to confront such an enormous obstacle? Or could Anse be one of those people whose physical expressions always seem inappropriate, like people who laugh when the occasion calls for tears?

Despite his look of pleasure, Anse is hesitant. Dewey Dell isn't, however. She looks at Tull the same way she looked at Samson, "her eyes . . . going hard like I had made to touch her." She's determined now to cross the river. She reminds Anse twice that "Mr Whitfield crossed it." Tull points out that Whitfield came across three days earlier, when the river was five feet lower.

Anse says that they'll probably be safe since he made his promise to Addie "in the presence of the Lord." But he is incapable of making a decision to cross.

As earlier, it is Jewel, the man of action, who makes the decisive move. Jewel snarls contemptuously at Tull before moving his horse and telling the family to "come on."

32. DARL

This section is a flashback. Read it for the insights it gives you into Jewel and Addie's special relationship.

NOTE: Flashbacks Faulkner uses flashbacks sparingly in this book. However, he does use them here, just before the crossing, and just after the crossing in sections 39, 40, and 41. The flashbacks deepen the meaning of the climactic crossing by telling us more about the characters—even the dead one, Addie. Also, by making you jump from the past to the present, the flashbacks are a kind of springboard that heightens the effects of the climax.

Three years earlier, Darl explains, when Jewel was 15, he took to sleeping on his feet. His mother and older brothers worried about him. He was losing weight.

It was when Addie began hiding things for Jewel to eat that Darl began to realize that the two had a special relationship. And he suspected that the relationship concealed a secret. Darl noticed Addie sitting in the dark next to Jewel when he was asleep. She was hating Jewel, Darl reasoned, for making her love him so much that she was forced to deceive others.

His older brothers realize that Jewel is staying out all night. Cash follows Jewel and discovers that he has been spending his nights clearing 40 acres of land for old Lon Quick.

One day Jewel rides up to the Bundrens' field with the spotted horse he bought with his earnings. Addie is there. She cries when she learns what happened.

NOTE: Addie's Relationship with Jewel What is the secret that this episode reveals to Darl? Why does Addie cry? And why does Jewel stare down at her from his horse, "his face growing cold and a little sick looking, until he looked away quick"?

These are all important questions—ones Faulkner raises here but does not answer directly. Some readers feel that Addie's tears are tears of relief over learning that Jewel is safe. Others feel that she cries so hard because she realizes that she is losing Jewel, that he is transferring his affections to the horse.

Perhaps—a third interpretation—he is declaring his independence here, not just from Addie but from the entire family. When he says he'll kill his horse before giving him Anse's feed, he's quite convincing.

---

33. TULL

Faulkner uses this section to build tension before the crossing. To understand his technique, look for images and observations that make you fear for the fate of the wagon.

Crossing the bridge with Vardaman, Dewey Dell, and Anse, Tull lists the visible dangers and suggests some not seen. The bridge is "shaking and swaying," its center dipping down into the "moiling" (muddily churning) water. Here Tull evokes an image of elemental forces emanating from inside the earth. Tull's group has to walk into the water before coming up on the other side. Those coming up on the other side, he suggests, look as if they "must come from the bottom of the earth."

Adding to the danger are logs floating down the river that bump against the sunken section of the bridge. The logs shoot "clean outen the water" and tumble on toward the ford—the point where the Bundrens hope to cross with the wagon.

From the far bank, Tull looks back at the wagon, which Cash is turning before bringing it down into the water. The wagon drops out of sight. For the life of him, Tull just can't figure out why the Bundrens would "risk the fire and the earth and the water" to get to Jefferson.

NOTE: Anse's Motivation   Faced with any obstacle, Anse is a jumble of weaknesses. Tull reminds you of them here. But what really seems to keep Anse going, more than the lure of new teeth, is his promise to Addie. "She is counting on it," he says. Anse's speaking of Addie as if she were alive calls attention to one of the novel's major themes: the ability of the dead to motivate the living.

34. DARL

Together, sections 34 to 36 will give you a complete picture of the crossing, which is the climax of the first portion of *As I Lay Dying*. Darl describes the crossing until the wagon begins to tip over halfway to the far bank.

His account is a dramatic one, although it builds slowly. They start across the river without any clear plan. Jewel takes the lead, a rope extended between the wagon and his saddle horn to brace the wagon against the current. His horse finds the ford—the old road beneath the river—and he beckons the others to come forward.

In the middle of the river, a huge log rises out of the water. The log is bearded with "a long gout of foam" and seems to walk on the water "like Christ." Compare this image with Cora's line in section 36: "Log, fiddlesticks. It was the hand of God." (See note, "Christian Imagery," in the discussion of section 36.)

As the log bears down on them, Cash does an odd thing. He reaches below the seat and unwinds the rope from its fastening, then tells Jewel to ride on and pull them ahead of the log. Jewel charges a good distance ahead before he realizes that the rope is free. Faulkner never explains this ruse on Cash's part. Can you?

The log strikes the wagon, tilting it. The mules lose their footing and drown. As the section ends,

Jewel is turning his horse violently in an attempt to get back to the wagon. Cash is trying to brace the coffin and his tool box. Darl has jumped off, to be carried by the current to shore.

NOTE: Images of Desolation   Darl describes the swollen river as a desolate place, a scene of barrenness and waste. Three times he refers to its "desolation." Its swiftness calls up an image of "the wasted world" accelerating "just before the final precipice." Such end-of-the-world imagery has led some readers to conclude that Faulkner is trying to evoke one of those mysterious rivers in Greek mythology that separates the world of the living from the world of the dead. One of those rivers that the souls of the dead were ferried across was the hateful Styx, the sacred river by whose name the gods took their most solemn oaths.

Does Faulkner mean to say that the Bundrens are crossing to the underworld—to the land of the dead? Or that they are returning from the underworld, as Tull suggested in section 33 when he said that people crossing the bridge seem as if they "must come from the bottom of the earth"?

Before you answer, remember how Faulkner uses ancient myths. He doesn't rewrite the old myths using modern characters. Instead, he makes references to the old myths to suggest stories that lend meaning to his own.

So you don't have to assume that the Bundrens are crossing to or from Hades—although you are free to. However, the link between a river in Mississippi and a river in Greek myth should make a bell go off in your mind. It should make you sit up and realize that, for the Bundrens, this crossing is terribly significant and treacherous.

35. VARDAMAN

Vardaman picks up the story where Darl left it—with Darl in the water and Cash trying to keep the coffin dry. Notice how Faulkner catches a young boy's excitement by omitting commas until the very end.

Vardaman's understanding of the scene is somewhat bent by his peculiar perspective. He thinks that his mother is a fish—"in the water she could go faster than a man"—and that Darl is in the water chasing her. Vardaman rushes down to the riverbank and is horrified to see Darl emerge from the water empty-handed.

The section ends with Vardaman running frantically along the bank. Faulkner maintains the suspense into the next section, where you will learn the outcome of the disaster.

36. TULL

Faulkner takes his time revealing how Addie and the wagon were saved. Before you discover what happened—from Tull's point of view—Faulkner has his characters explore some of the Christian imagery that he suggested earlier.

NOTE: Christian Imagery Readers who examined the original manuscript of *As I Lay Dying* discovered that Faulkner penciled in as an afterthought the sentence about the log's rising upright "like Christ." His biographer, Joseph Blotner, believes that Faulkner may have added the reference to Christ in order to prepare you for Cora's calling the log "the hand of God" in this section.

Why would he want to do that? There are at least two possibilities you might explore. First, Faulkner might share Cora's view—that, as Vernon says, the Bundrens "was daring the hand of God to try" the crossing. It's a perfectly acceptable interpretation of the event, and not just to someone who, like Cora, takes her religion literally. As has been noted, Faulkner alludes to several Biblical and Greek myths in which characters defy the gods.

Tull describes his view of the disaster in the river. He sees Darl jumping from the wagon as it turns over and Cash fighting to keep the coffin from slipping. In the end, Jewel and his horse are the heroes of the day. The horse pulls Cash out of the water. Jewel has managed to fasten his rope to the wagon and keep it—and Addie's coffin on top of it—from being pulled downstream by the current.

37. DARL

Darl describes the aftermath of the disaster, as the family tries to recover on the far bank of the river. He provides a touching look at the solidarity of the Bundrens and their helpful neighbor, Vernon Tull.

It's an hour after the crossing. Cash lies still on the ground. The wagon has been hauled ashore, the coffin still lying "profoundly" on the wagon bed.

NOTE: A Violent Presence   In an aside, Darl tells why the family chocked the wheels of the wagon carefully. On the wagon, it seems, "there lingered somehow . . . that violence which had slain the mules. . . ." The only thing on the wagon is Addie in her coffin. Could Faulkner be suggesting that there's something violent about Addie's character we have yet to learn about?

Vernon and Jewel dive for Cash's tools. Vardaman, Darl, and even Dewey Dell help. Anse just stands and watches, mournfully, now and then walking down to gaze at his dead mules. As they find the tools, one after another, they set them down beside Cash like offerings. Toward the end of the chapter, you learn that Cash's leg is broken.

NOTE: Dewey Dell and the Earth   The section ends with a passage that identifies Dewey Dell, once again, with the fertility of the earth. Her "wet dress shapes . . . those mammalian ludicrosities which are the horizons and the valleys of the earth."

38. CASH
After spending a section describing Cash's visible anguish, Faulkner composes this brief and sudden section like the punch line of a joke. Lying there, you realize, Cash's concerns are not at all those of his family. His concerns are personal: an obsession with his craft, and with the way the coffin failed to balance properly on the wagon. Brief

as it is, the section buttresses the novel's theme that people are isolated from one another even when they are united in a common purpose.

39. CORA

Sections 39 to 41 are flashbacks. Faulkner takes your attention away from the journey while Cora, Addie, and Whitfield reminisce. The three sections are tied together as a unit. Notice, as you read them, how each one introduces the next and comments on the others.

Almost from the start, Cora sounds like Elihu—the fourth speaker in the Book of Job who accuses Job of arrogant pride. Cora believes that Addie takes "God's love and her duty to Him too much as a matter of course, and such conduct is not pleasing to Him." When Addie says, "My daily life is an acknowledgment and expiation of my sin," Cora explodes. "Who are you, to say what is sin and what is not sin? It is the Lord's part to judge; ours to praise His mercy. . . ."

She doesn't stop to ask—as you should—what Addie's sin is. Instead, she shoots ahead, missing the point. "Just because you have been a faithful wife is no sign that there is no sin in your heart," she says. "I know my own sin," Addie says. "I know that I deserve my punishment."

Again, Cora has too much momentum going to ask—as you should—what that punishment is. Addie's sin, Cora feels, is favoring Jewel instead of Darl, and her punishment is not having that love returned. "Jewel is your punishment," she says. "But where is your salvation?"

Watch how Addie replies. "He is my cross and

he will be my salvation," she says. (By "cross," she means her burden—not her sin. The reference is to the cross that Christ carried to his crucifixion.) "He will save me from the water and from the fire," she goes on. "Even though I have laid down my life, he will save me." Addie is of course speaking of Jewel.

NOTE: Cora's Confusion   Addie's boast that Jewel will be her salvation echoes two lines from the 66th Psalm in the Old Testament. "We went through fire and through water; but thou [God] brought us out into a wealthy place." The next line is a paraphrase of a section of the 23rd Psalm: "Though I walk through the valley of death, I fear no evil, for thou [God] art with me."

Cora thinks Addie is referring to God and not to Jewel. When she realizes her mistake, she is dumbfounded. She is sure that Addie is mocking God—that "she had spoken sacrilege." It's a confirmation of all Cora's fears: Addie is "lost in her vanity and her pride" and has "closed her heart to God and set that selfish mortal boy in His place."

Cora views "Brother Whitfield"—"a godly man"—as her ally. She talks about "that summer at the camp meeting" when Whitfield "wrestled with [Addie's] spirit, singled her out and strove with her vanity in her mortal heart."

NOTE: Camp Meetings   Camp meetings were popular in the 19th and early 20th centuries. They were revival meetings, when families set up tents in the country for a couple of weeks and mixed vacation with religion. Evidently Whitfield spent a lot of time with Addie at one such gathering.

What do you think about Cora's report? Do you think that Addie's sin is loving Jewel, and that her punishment is not getting his love in return?

Addie makes clear in the next section that she has another sort of sin in mind. She is not so clear about her punishment.

Some readers think that maybe Cora is on to something when she says, "Jewel is your punishment." Does Addie seem to agree with Cora when she compares Jewel to the cross Christ had to bear?

NOTE: Sin in *As I Lay Dying* It's not always easy to figure out just what Faulkner's people mean when they talk about sin. Actually, they're talking about two sorts of sin: (1) the sin of the human race, traceable to Adam's original sin; and (2) personal sin. According to the Bible, Adam was the first man. His sin—the original sin—was to eat the fruit of the tree of knowledge in the Garden of Eden. For this disobedient act, Adam was banished from the Garden of Eden, together with Eve, who tempted him to eat the fruit. Adam's sin left all humans with a tendency to sin, or act unethically, requiring constant vigilance on the part of the individual.

As to personal sin, some Christians divide all human acts into good, indifferent, or bad. Faulkner's people, like most conservative Christians, believe that all acts that are not positively good are sinful. There can be no indifferent act. Thus, to

Cora, favoring Jewel over her other children is sinful. An even worse sin is idolatry—setting up a human in God's place. It is precisely this sin that Cora feels Addie commits. The sin brings Cora to her knees, begging God to forgive Addie and redeem her, or deliver her from sin.

Christians call that deliverance "salvation." Addie is convinced that Jewel will be her salvation—not realizing, perhaps, that he would save her quite literally. Another irony is that when he "saves" her, she is already dead—beyond physical, if not spiritual, salvation.

40. ADDIE

Many readers find this section the most revealing one in the novel. It is Addie's only monologue, and it ties together a lot of the novel's loose ends.

Addie begins with a reminiscence of her days teaching school. She was unhappy as a teacher, because like all children her pupils were self-absorbed. She hated them. She whipped them eagerly when they made mistakes.

What did she mean by that viciousness? What was her aim? Some readers feel that she was lonely, and that she hoped to break through her isolation by inflicting pain. "I would think with each blow of the switch: Now you are aware of me! Now I am something in your secret and selfish life. . . ."

NOTE: "And so I took Anse" Like most interior monologues, this one is replete with non sequiturs—passages that don't seem to follow previous ones with any logic. (In Latin, *non sequitur* means

"It does not follow.") One of the most baffling of these is the line, "And so I took Anse." Addie says it twice—the second time without the *and*—as a frame for the story of the courtship that led to her marriage.

Many readers think the line important. Addie does not say, "And so I fell in love with Anse," or, "And so I married Anse." So some readers feel that she saw Anse only as an object, like the switch she scarred her pupils with, and hoped to use him to break through her isolation.

But Anse never "violated" her "aloneness." It took Cash, her first-born, to do that.

In this section Faulkner explores at length one of the novel's major themes, the futility of words compared with actions. Words, to Addie, are without value. "Words go straight up in a thin line, quick and harmless," she says. The word *love*, "like the others," is "just a shape to fill a lack." Anse used the word *love* to describe what Addie knew didn't exist—real love between them.

With Cash, it was different. The love between mother and son was very strong, something both of them experienced. "Cash did not need to say it [the word *love*] to me nor I to him."

Obviously, action—something which is experienced, not just talked about—is the test of life to Addie. If something cannot be experienced, it cannot be alive. Thus, Anse is dead to her, just a word, "a significant shape profoundly without life."

Having Cash didn't end Addie's isolation. It only intensified it, leaving "time, Anse, love"—everything without meaning to her—"outside the circle" of her loneliness.

Darl was an unwanted child. When Addie learned she was pregnant with Darl, she was furious. She felt Anse had tricked her. So she decided to get revenge. She made Anse promise to bury her in Jefferson when she died.

NOTE: Addie's Mean-spiritedness   To some readers, these revelations help explain a couple of the novel's mysteries. Many readers trace Darl's oddness to the fact that his mother shunned him. According to this interpretation, Darl's rejection causes him to wonder if he exists, and it eventually drives him out of his mind.

Addie's concocting the journey to Jefferson as a form of revenge against Anse adds another dramatic irony to the novel. Suddenly you realize what Addie's survivors don't: that Addie may not have cared at all about being buried in Jefferson. Anse, Dewey Dell, and Vardaman have personal errands pulling them to Jefferson. Now we realize that Addie also had an ulterior motive—revenge.

It's a strange form of revenge. When you're getting back at someone, you want that person to know it. Not Addie. As she says, Anse "would never know I was taking revenge."

What do these revelations make you think about Addie?

In the final segment of the monologue, Addie describes her affair with Whitfield. This infidelity amounted to a series of passionate trysts in the woods, probably during the camp meeting that Cora refers to in section 39.

To some readers, her adultery was a defiant, rebellious act. To others, it was an attempt to reach outside of herself and experience the "terrible blood" of reality through sin—a "more utter and terrible" sin because it was committed with a minister.

Whatever the reason for it, the affair was Addie's sin. Jewel—in her view—was her punishment. Yet, she saw her redemption in the affair, too. Talking with Cora, you will remember, Addie called Jewel her "cross" *and* her "salvation."

NOTE: Parallels with *The Scarlet Letter*   You might enjoy playing with the similarities many readers find between *As I Lay Dying* and Nathaniel Hawthorne's masterpiece, *The Scarlet Letter*, written in 1850. *The Scarlet Letter* explores through allegory and symbolism the problems of moral evil and guilt. The heroine, Hester Prynne, is, like Addie, caught in a loveless marriage to a man with a physical deformity. (Hester's husband has a twisted shoulder; Addie's, a humped back.) Hester has an adulterous affair with her minister—a man named Dimmesdale who, like Whitfield, is highly respected by his community. Hester names the child of this sin Pearl—her jewel. Both Hester and Addie despise deceit but practice it to protect their lovers.

After Jewel's birth, Addie put her affairs in order—she "cleaned [her] house." She made amends to Anse by giving him two more children, Dewey Dell and Vardaman. (She always considered Dewey

Dell, Vardaman, and Darl to be Anse's children, not hers.) This done, she "could get ready to die."

41. WHITFIELD

This section ends the flashbacks that began with Cora's soliloquy. It presents a picture of the sort of religiosity and emptiness of words that Addie detests.

Faulkner structures this section as a simple narrative. Whitfield hears that Addie is dying, and God tells him to confess his adultery to Anse. He risks his life to reach the Bundrens' house.

When he learns from one of the Tulls' daughters that Addie has died, he changes his mind about confessing. God, he reasons, "will accept the will for the deed."

He enters the Bundrens' "lowly dwelling" cleansed of doubt. "God's grace upon this house," he says.

NOTE: Whitfield's Prayer   Read Whitfield's prayer aloud, and you will hear echoes of Psalms in the Old Testament. His prayer imitates the repetitive structure of those poetic pieces. Whitfield says "let me not" three times and "let not" twice. Pick up a Bible and leaf through the Book of Psalms, and you will find similar devices used there.

It is fitting that a man of the cloth should speak in biblical cadences—after all, he is probably more familiar with the Bible than with any other piece of literature. However, Faulkner may have another purpose in framing Whitfield's thoughts this way. He may be indicating that Whitfield is a phony, talking in a voice that is not his own.

Back in section 20, Tull suggested as much. Whitfield's voice as he presided over Addie's funeral didn't seem to be part of him.

Some readers think this section funny. Whether you do or not will depend on your view of Whitfield. You may think him contemptuous—someone to sneer at, not laugh at. On the other hand, you may see him as a sort of clown, a weakling who thinks he can trick even God into believing he is strong and blameless. A clown's hypocrisy is usually harmless. A villain's is not. You can laugh at Charlie Chaplin but not at Adolf Hitler. Which sort of a hypocrite is Whitfield?

How could Addie fall for such an empty person? This is one of the many mysteries of *As I Lay Dying* that Faulkner invites you to solve. Was Addie blind to Whitfield's weaknesses? Or was her passion for him totally physical and his weaknesses of no significance to her?

42. DARL

This section brings you back to the present, and to the interrupted journey. Darl's narration gets more complex here, as his attention switches without warning from the general action to Jewel. References to Jewel are printed in italics.

As the section opens, Jewel rides back to the riverbank leading a team he has borrowed from Henry Armstid, a farmer who lives nearby. Vernon leaves to recross the bridge as the family drives off to Armstid's farm with Cash lying on top of Addie's coffin.

The dunking helped cut down the smell of the

rotting body. Armstid offers to let Anse put the coffin in the house overnight. Anse refuses the offer and stores the wagon and coffin in a one-sided shed. Lula Armstid feeds them and puts Cash to bed inside the house.

Darl's description of Jewel's activities seems to indicate a certain obsession on Darl's part. After you've read the entire section, go back and read through just the italicized passages to see what fascinates Darl about Jewel. We see Jewel continually in motion—on his horse and off it, taking care of it. Jewel doesn't even leave his horse to go into the Armstid's house to eat.

43. ARMSTID

Armstid's only monologue is a tricky one. And that's what makes it a fine demonstration of Faulkner's mastery of the storyteller's art. He reveals what's happening in bits and pieces, leaving you in doubt until the next to last paragraph. In the last paragraph, he raises a question about Jewel that keeps you turning pages to find an answer.

Basically, this chapter is about Anse's search for a team to replace the one that drowned during the river crossing. But other things happen during the nearly two days the Bundrens stay at the Armstids'. Jewel can't locate Peabody to fix Cash's leg, so Uncle Billy sets Cash's leg with the help of Jewel and Dewey Dell. Though Cash faints, he never complains.

Addie's body has begun to smell again. The smell draws buzzards, and Vardaman spends most of his time chasing them away. The smell prompts Lula Armstid to express her outrage over the way the Bundrens are treating Addie.

Lula's outrage moves Armstid to ask Jewel if he wants to borrow a mule to look for Anse, who has ridden off on Jewel's horse to buy a mule team from a man named Snopes. Jewel explodes, knowing that Armstid wants the smell out of his yard. He is so mad he shakes "like he had a aguer"—a fever. Jewel tries to move the wagon out of the shed but is unable to budge it. Darl refuses to help him.

Anse returns in the evening. He has made a deal for a mule team. After much prying, he is forced to admit that he offered Jewel's horse in return.

NOTE: Cash's Money   While trying to guess what Anse exchanged for the team, Darl remembers Anse's going through Cash's clothes the night before. Apparently Anse stole eight dollars from Cash—not enough, Darl realizes, to buy a team. Anse's action—stealing from his own son—is another clue to his selfish character. Equally interesting, however, is Darl's statement that Cash intended to spend the money in Jefferson on a "talking machine" (a graphophone). So Cash had a personal reason to go to Jefferson, too!

Jewel is dumbfounded to learn that Anse offered his horse in trade for a mule team. He leaps on the horse and takes off like "a spotted cyclone." Anse borrows Armstid's team to haul the wagon (with Cash on top) about a mile down the road.

The next morning, one of Snopes' farmhands appears at Armstid's house with a team of mules for Anse. The farmhand found Jewel's horse in

Snopes' barn that morning. Apparently Jewel had ridden it there, sacrificing his prize possession.

NOTE: Jewel's Sacrifice   Jewel's sacrifice is one more demonstration of his love for Addie. It should remind you of Addie's prophecy—that Jewel will be her "salvation."

---

44. VARDAMAN

Faulkner reports events from a child's perspective again in this section. Note, as you read it, how an innocent eye can misinterpret—or fail to interpret—events.

NOTE: Symbol of the Buzzards   The vultures that follow the Bundrens throughout their journey are a constant reminder of death. In a real sense, these black carrion-eaters stand for death—a haunting symbol of the end that awaits everyone, not just Addie. Vardaman is fascinated by them. He issues periodic reports of their numbers in this section.

Vardaman still believes his mother to be a fish. He won't believe she is inside the coffin, although Dewey Dell has apparently tried to persuade him that she is. Darl, more thoughtful and imaginative than Dewey Dell, has told Vardaman that he might see Addie when they reach water again.

Cash is in pain but uncomplaining. "Don't bother none," he tells Darl. Anse figures they'll "just have to" buy medicine in Mottson, a small town they are heading toward.

Vardaman can't understand why Jewel is gone. He wonders if his departure has something to do with Jewel's mother's being a horse. Darl never answers that question. If it were addressed to you, how would you answer it?

45. MOSELEY

This section provides you with another "outside opinion" of the Bundrens. Moseley, who owns a drug store in Mottson, reminds you just how bizarre the journey is.

Moseley sees Dewey Dell looking into his shop through the window. Before entering, she "kind of bumbled at the screen door a minute, like they do," he says. The word *they* refers not just to the Bundrens but to the class of people—hill farmers—from which they spring. The gap between town people and hill people is a recurrent theme in the novel.

Moseley can't get Dewey Dell to tell him what it is she wants. When he learns that she wants something to induce an abortion, he is indignant. He advises Dewey Dell to use the ten dollars Lafe gave her to get married.

After Dewey Dell leaves, Albert, Moseley's assistant, describes the scene on the street. Anse parked in front of the hardware store, and the smell of Addie's body, dead eight days, made women flee. But Anse won't move on. "It's a public street," he tells a marshal.

NOTE: Yoknapatawpha County Albert tells Moseley that the Bundrens "came from some place out in Yoknapatawpha county." This is the first

mention in any of Faulkner's books of the name
he gave the county where 15 of his novels are set.
Faulkner called the county his "mythical kingdom." Yet its geography and history parallel in
many ways those of Lafayette County, in northern
Mississippi, where he lived most of his life.

It wasn't until he wrote his third novel, *Sartoris*,
in 1928, that he began to mine this region for material for his books. He finally realized, he said
later, that "my own little postage stamp of native
soil was worth writing about and that I would never
live long enough to exhaust it, and that by subli-
mating the actual into the apocryphal I would have
complete liberty to use whatever talent I might have
to its absolute top."

Faulkner said the name comes from the Chick-
asaw words *yocana* and *petopha*, which mean "water
runs slow through flat land." Faulkner made Yoknapatawpha County the most famous region in
American literature. He drew a map of the county
for *The Portable Faulkner*, edited by Malcolm Cowley.

46. DARL

For the most part, this section describes the family mixing cement and fashioning a cast for Cash's
leg. As you read it, notice how Darl's mind seems
to come apart.

Cash doesn't want them to delay the journey for
his sake. And when they apply the cement to his
leg, his only worry is that it will drip onto the
coffin.

The most remarkable thing about this section is
Darl's behavior. In the last section, the druggist's
assistant told how Darl came out of the hardware

store and ordered Anse to shut up. That outburst may have seemed uncharacteristic to you. Here, Darl is harsh with Anse again. When Anse says he doesn't want to "be beholden" to anyone for a bucket and water, Darl says, "Then make some water yourself."

Moreover, Darl pitches in with the rest to make a cement cast—something that will certainly do more harm than good. For the first time, he proves as ignorant about something as the rest of the family.

Meanwhile, his mind seems momentarily to lose its focus in two places. The imagery of these poetic passages is of weariness, of lives that wind out into nothingness. What is Darl saying when he ponders how nice it would be "if you could just ravel out into time"? Is he talking about an alternative to death and burial? Or might he be longing to escape the world he finds himself in?

At the end of the chapter, Jewel reappears, moving rigidly and without a word, and climbs onto the wagon.

47. VARDAMAN

Vardaman tries to make sense of his jigsaw-puzzle world by fitting the pieces together in his mind. His fixation on the vultures interrupts his thoughts. He looks forward to seeing where the vultures spend the night. It's an innocent desire, and one which will put him in a position to witness a crime.

48. DARL

Stopping at the Gillespies' farm for the night, the Bundrens put Addie's coffin under an apple tree. There, Darl seems to slip further into a private world. He hears Addie talk "in little trickling bursts." And he teases Jewel about his paternity. "Who was your father, Jewel?"

Why do you suppose he persists with his taunts? Is he just being malicious, trying to get a rise out of a rival? Or might he be trying to force Jewel to come to terms with his parentage—and his own relationship to the surviving members of the family?

It's unclear who speaks to Cash and soothes his leg with water. Darl assigns many of the statements and actions to "we"—the family—instead of to individual members. In this way, Faulkner may be underscoring the unity of the family which Jewel has rejected.

49. VARDAMAN

In this complicated section, Faulkner prepares you for the book's climactic scene. Notice how he builds tension with the two italicized flash-forwards that interrupt Vardaman's description of what's going on around him.

Darl shows Vardaman how to listen to Addie by putting his ear close to the coffin. Darl explains that Addie is "talking to God . . . calling on Him to help her." Addie wants God to "hide her away from the sight of man," he says.

What do you think Darl means by this? Faulkner does not waste words in this book, so chances are good that these are not throwaway lines. Many readers feel that this is Darl's way of saying that the journey has gone on far enough.

You'll have to make up your own mind as to whether Darl actually hears Addie talk. If he does hear voices, he may be insane—more than just "queer," as his neighbors call him.

Dewey Dell and Vardaman sleep on the Gillespies' porch, facing the yard. The wind shifts, bringing the smell of Addie's body to the house. The men move the coffin into the barn. Dewey Dell falls asleep, and Vardaman sneaks off to the barn to see where the vultures sleep. And that's where he witnesses something that Dewey Dell has told him not to tell anybody.

50. DARL

Jewel fulfills Addie's prophecy in this section, the novel's major climax. The scene is a fine example of Faulkner's ability to involve you in action.

Faulkner begins the episode in medias res—"in the middle of things." Jewel is in motion from the first sentence to the last. Darl is outside the house—a clue that he may have caused the emergency. He spots Jewel leaping out of the house, the glare of the fire reflected in his eyes.

Inside the burning barn, Jewel pauses at the coffin and looks back furiously at Darl. He and Darl and the other men rescue the animals.

The animals saved, Jewel heads back into the barn for the coffin. Gillespie tries to stop him but cannot. Jewel knocks Gillespie down and races into the barn. With a superhuman effort, Jewel—"enclosed in a thin nimbus of fire," like a god—carries Addie's coffin to safety.

NOTE: Allusion to Greek Myth   Darl describes Gillespie, who is naked, and Jewel, who is in his underwear, as "like two figures in a Greek frieze, isolated out of all reality by the red glare." A frieze is a relief sculpture that appears on many ancient buildings. Greek friezes often portrayed warriors in combat. By making this reference, Faulkner suggests once more that his characters have a mythical dimension, one that makes them "larger than life."

51. VARDAMAN

Vardaman describes the fire's aftermath. Cash's foot has turned black. The men try to chip off the cast but succeed only in cracking it.

Jewel lies on his stomach, his back raw. Under the apple tree, Darl is lying on the coffin, weeping.

Why is he crying? Vardaman assumes it is because Addie was almost lost in the fire. But he might be crying from relief, or even because he is insane. He might be crying *for* Addie, because she did not burn and must bear the agony of continuing the journey.

52. DARL

The funeral cortege finally reaches Jefferson in this section. Darl describes the family's exhaustion as they approach the town. Everyone is thinner, including Vardaman.

The town seems to breathe life back into the family. When Jewel speaks angrily about digging "a damn hole in the ground," Anse puts on his old airs and once more shows his ignorance of his children's feelings. "You never pure loved her, none of you," he says. What might Addie say about his use of the word *love*?

Dewey Dell has Anse stop the wagon outside of town. She disappears into the bushes and reappears wearing her Sunday clothes, which she had been carrying wrapped in newspaper.

The smell of Addie's corpse outrages people they pass on the hill into town. Reacting to their outrage, Jewel nearly provokes a fight. Darl convinces Jewel to apologize.

NOTE: Darl's Mind   Darl seems very much in control here, a marked contrast to his erratic focus in earlier sections. This is a useful point to remember, because his sanity will become an issue in the next section.

---

53. CASH

The Cash that Faulkner presents here may surprise you. He appears here and in the final section as one of the novel's most thoughtful characters.

NOTE: Darl's Sanity   How sane is Darl? Cash tries to answer that question in this section. He decides, as members of any farm community might, that anyone who would set fire to a barn and endanger livestock must be crazy. He balances this judgment with understanding, however. "I can almost believe he done right in a way," he says. He can see how Darl could think it was necessary to "get shut of her in some clean way."

Is Darl insane enough to warrant being committed to an asylum? Psychiatrists would no doubt disagree. It's a moot point, because, as Cash says, "It was either send him to Jackson, or have Gillespie sue us." Anse would rather see his son behind bars than pay for Gillespie's barn.

Anse borrows two shovels, and the family buries Addie. Faulkner handles her burial almost as an afterthought. Can you suggest why?

What surprises Cash most about the way Darl is taken is Dewey Dell's violence toward him. She leaps on Darl, "scratching and clawing . . . like a wild cat." Her hatred for Darl, who knows her secret, leads Cash to conclude that it was she who told the Gillespies that Darl set their barn on fire.

Like Dewey Dell, Jewel uses the occasion to vent his anger. "Kill him. Kill the son of a bitch," Jewel yells.

Darl's reaction is pitiful. Lying on his back, pinned down, he looks up at Cash and says, "I thought you would have told me." Later he sits on the ground, laughing. When Cash tells him Jackson will be "better for you, Darl," Darl plays with the word *better* and continues to laugh.

Would an asylum be better for Darl—"quiet, with none of the bothering and such," as Cash tells him? Or would he just be exchanging one lunatic world for another?

NOTE: "Mrs Bundren"   Cash's reference to Mrs. Bundren is misleading. Cash is not speaking of Addie, or her people, but of the woman who will soon become Anse's second wife.

---

54. PEABODY

Doc Peabody's second (and final) monologue contains none of the philosophizing of his first one. He is laboring over Cash's leg shortly after Addie's burial. Cash stands to end up with a shortened leg—one he may never be able to walk on again.

Anse, who is off returning the spades, takes the brunt of Peabody's anger. Notice how Peabody compares him to a disease that has infected the entire family. Is his diagnosis accurate?

Peabody seems sickened that Darl was handcuffed "like a damn murderer." But what angers him more, it appears, is that the action didn't bother Anse.

55. MacGOWAN

In this comic monologue, Skeet MacGowan, a druggist's assistant, takes advantage of Dewey Dell's ignorance and desperation. Her search for an abortion is the first of the Bundrens' personal errands whose results Faulkner must report on before he can end the novel.

MacGowan clearly thinks he is pretty clever and that women—especially country women—are beneath him. Today you might call him sexist, a term that Faulkner never knew. Most of his monologue is a braggart's description of how he seduced a gullible stranger. Faulkner makes the action move swiftly, and he even adds some tension by keeping one of MacGowan's eyes on the clock.

NOTE: MacGowan's Comic Mask Dewey Dell is a mere object to MacGowan, as she might be to any listener who didn't know her. But you do know her—"warts" and all—and that fact may make you less amused than MacGowan with his conquest.

Still, MacGowan is a comic figure. Note the role his wise-guy patter plays in making him funny, and note, too, his ignorance—of grammar, pharmacology, and even of Dewey Dell. Also observe his position in the shop. When you meet him, he's doing a mundane task, pouring chocolate syrup, and he continually eyes the clock to make sure his boss won't catch him. He is really a clown—more pathetic than heroic—despite what *he* would like you, his listener, to believe.

---

56. VARDAMAN

In the previous section, MacGowan spotted Vardaman sitting on the curb outside the drugstore. Here, Vardaman accompanies his sister to and from her meeting with MacGowan.

Vardaman displays a country boy's fascination with the town. The street lights "roosting in the trees" intrigue him. A cow clops through town as Vardaman waits for Dewey Dell to emerge from the drugstore, and his senses are so alert he even "hears" the silences between hoofbeats. When the cow leaves the square, he is aware as never before of the square's emptiness—an objective correlative which signals his loneliness.

The town's sights and sounds don't blot out Vardaman's thoughts of Darl and the electric train he came to Jefferson to see. The two thoughts are united by the image of a train—the one Darl took to Jackson, and the one he still hopes to see in the store window.

Apparently they've already made a visit to the toy store and learned that its owner won't display the train until Christmas. Vardaman has had to settle for a substitute—a "bag full" of bananas, which he will share with Dewey Dell.

When Dewey Dell leaves the drugstore, she is angry. She is sure that MacGowan has tricked her. Like Vardaman, she's not going to get what she came to Jefferson for.

57. DARL

Darl's final monologue is perhaps the most difficult one to make sense of. Separated from his family, he seems to have lost touch with reality.

Apparently inside the asylum at Jackson, Darl recalls leaving Jefferson by train with two armed guards. Thoughts of incest and bestiality clash in his mind and make him laugh. We learn for the first time that he went to France during World War I.

There is also an ending here, and a beginning. The journey to Jefferson is over. Two journeys from Jefferson have begun. Darl has gone to Jackson. His family is about to depart for home. It could just be, some readers think, that Darl is a kind of crazed Janus—the god of endings and beginnings—overseeing both journeys.

Is Darl insane? Some readers insist that he is just acting the part that others have thrust upon him. Darl is laughing at the absurd world he is escaping, they say. Others insist that Darl is insane, and that his family's rejection of him—after Addie's painful rejection—finally pushed him over the edge.

58. DEWEY DELL

Dewey Dell's final monologue provides another damning glimpse of Anse in action. He has discovered her ten-dollar bill and wants it. Dewey Dell tells him not to touch it. This outburst gives Anse another chance to exhibit his self-pity. In the end, he gets what he wants—which is, as usual, something that belongs to someone else.

NOTE: It's not clear when this scene takes place. The next section suggests that it occurred the morning after Dewey Dell's meeting with Mac-Gowan.

---

59. CASH

Cash has the last word. He describes the family's final moments in Jefferson.

After the burial and Darl's capture, Anse returns the shovels to the widow's house. He goes back to her house in the evening and apparently spends the night there. Peabody has given the family enough money to stay in a hotel.

In the morning, after asking Cash for money—and probably taking Dewey Dell's—he buys a set of teeth and gets married. Jewel, Dewey Dell, Vardaman, and Cash are outside the courthouse when Anse arrives sheepishly with his new wife, a "duck-shaped woman" with "pop eyes." To Cash's delight, she is carrying a graphophone, a wind-up phonograph. So, he and Anse, of all the Bundrens, get what they'd hoped to get in Jefferson.

The next-to-last paragraph adds a bittersweet note. Cash regrets that Darl can't enjoy the graphophone, too. But, he says, "This world is not his world; this life his life."

Anse's introduction of his new wife to his children ends the novel on an upbeat note. Looking "hangdog and proud," he tells his children, "Meet Mrs Bundren." The book ends with a smile and perhaps even with some hope.

NOTE: Summing Up   What are we to make of this story? One way to approach the answer would be to draw a balance sheet. What did the Bundrens lose and what did they gain from the journey? The losses can be toted up quickly: two dead mules, Jewel's horse, Cash's crippled leg, and Darl's institutionalization.

The gains aren't so easily added up. Although Cash got his graphophone, the visible gains were mainly Anse's: new teeth and a wife. Yet even Darl, if you choose to believe Cash, will be better off. Moreover, the fact that Anse profited from the journey means that Addie never got her revenge.

Toting up the gains and losses, some readers have concluded that the book sounds a hopeful note. They see in the battered family's survival a victory for the human race, whose next generation Dewey Dell was unable to abort. Twenty years after writing *As I Lay Dying*, Faulkner spoke in these terms when he accepted the Nobel Prize for Literature. "I believe that man will not merely endure he will prevail," he said. "He is immortal, not because he alone among creatures has an inexhaustible voice, but because he has a soul, a spirit capable of compassion and sacrifice and endurance."

A STEP BEYOND

Tests and Answers

TESTS

Test 1

1. The major themes of *As I Lay Dying* are _____
   I. the uselessness of words when separated from action
   II. the control the living have over the dead
   III. the individual's isolation from others within a community
      A. I, II, and III   B. II and III only
      C. I and III only

2. Addie married Anse in hopes of _____
   A. finding someone to support her
   B. having someone break through her shell of solitude
   C. testing her ability to withstand hardship

3. Jewel's name symbolizes the fact that he is _____
   A. the product of a costly transgression
   B. Addie's favorite child
   C. modeled after Hester Prynne's daughter Pearl

4. Cora Tull accuses Addie of the sin of _____
   A. pride   B. lust   C. anger

5. A major difference between Anse and Cash is _____

    A. Anse suffers in silence, Cash suffers
       aloud
    B. Anse suffers aloud, Cash suffers in
       silence
    C. Anse is selfless, Cash is selfish

6. After Darl's birth, Addie made Anse prom-   _____
   ise to
   A. never get her pregnant again
   B. stop risking his health by overworking
   C. bury her in Jefferson

7. Anse agreed to have Darl committed to the   _____
   insane asylum because he
   A. wanted to avoid paying for Gillespie's
      barn
   B. feared that Darl might harm Anse's
      new wife
   C. agreed with Doc Peabody that Darl
      was insane

8. The son whose actions justified his moth-   _____
   er's faith in him was
   A. Cash   B. Vardaman   C. Jewel

9. Rachel Samson and Lula Armstid are both   _____
   outraged by
   A. their husbands' lack of hospitality
      toward the Bundrens
   B. the way the surviving Bundrens treat
      Addie's corpse
   C. Anse's trading the horse of Addie's
      favorite son for two mules

10. Darl's most unusual power is his ability to   _____
    A. convince the family to work together
    B. observe scenes that take place miles
       away

C. make even his closest relatives wish
him dead

11. How might Addie's attitude toward her children at
their birth shape their attitudes toward her at her
death?

12. How does Faulkner use Whitfield and Cora Tull to
advance the theme that words divorced from experience are worthless?

13. What views do the townspeople and country folk
hold of each other?

14. Discuss the surviving Bundrens as examples of what
Peabody means when he says that death is "merely
a function of the mind—and that of the minds of
the ones who suffer the bereavement."

Test 2

1. Anse wants to go to Jefferson to   _____
   A. fulfill his promise to Addie
   B. get some false teeth
   C. both A and B

2. For Cash, making Addie's coffin is   _____
   A. a chore he finds hard to perform
   B. the way he shows his love for his
   mother
   C. both A and B

3. Faulkner uses people outside the family as   _____
   narrators in order to
   A. provide an objective view of the
   Bundrens
   B. suggest the presence of a Greek
   chorus

C. give the Bundrens the chance to
   bounce their ideas off other people

4. Vardaman at first blames his mother's death _____
   on
   A. a fish   B. the Tulls' horses
   C. Doc Peabody

5. The sulphur in the air around the Bun- _____
   drens' home suggests
   A. death by fire
   B. the underworld in Greek and
      Christian myth
   C. the presence of a nearby sulphur mine

6. Addie had Dewey Dell and Vardaman in _____
   order to
   A. make amends to Anse for having
      Jewel
   B. violate her aloneness
   C. provide some insurance against old
      age

7. The buzzards that follow the Bundrens to _____
   Jefferson act as a reminder and a symbol of
   A. death   B. the Bundrens' isolation
   C. both A and B

8. The secret that Dewey Dell tells Vardaman _____
   not to reveal involves
   A. Addie's affair with Whitfield
   B. Dewey Dell's pregnancy
   C. Darl's setting Gillespie's barn on fire

9. When he marries the second Mrs. Bundren, Anse inadvertently fulfills Cash's goal of   _____
   A. eating a bag of bananas
   B. bringing a graphophone into the house
   C. replacing his mother

10. Jewel expresses himself best through   _____
    A. language   B. silence   C. action

11. Discuss Faulkner's view of women in *As I Lay Dying*.

12. How does Faulkner use Greek myth in the novel?

13. In what ways could *As I Lay Dying* be described as a comic novel?

14. What events show Jewel the way Addie describes him to Cora: as her "cross" and her "salvation"?

ANSWERS

Test 1

1. C   **2.** B   **3.** B   **4.** A   **5.** B   **6.** C
7. A   **8.** C   **9.** B   **10.** B

11. The way Addie felt about her children at their birth is mirrored in the way they feel about themselves and her. Reread Addie's monologue (section 40) to refresh your memory about her feelings. She loved Cash, her firstborn. She rejected Darl, thinking him the unwanted product of unfelt love. Jewel, her favorite, was the result of her life's major passion. She had Dewey Dell, Addie says, to "negative" Jewel, and Vardaman "to replace the child I had robbed [Anse] of."

Cash responds to her love with a symbolic offering of love: the coffin which he made so carefully. (See sections 1, 12.) Rejected by Addie, the "motherless" Darl wonders if he exists and perpetuates a sibling rivalry with Jewel.

Jewel, the symbol of her passionate affair with Whitfield, responds to her death with passion. In section 4, he has a fantasy of being her violent protector. He rescues her body twice (sections 36 and 50).

Dewey Dell seems moved the least by Addie's death, perhaps because Addie conceived of her only as an object—something to negate Jewel. Vardaman, who was conceived as a replacement for Jewel, in turn replaces Addie—in his mind, at least—with a fish.

12. Review Addie's monologue (section 40) for her view of words as an inadequate substitute for experience. To see how Whitfield separates words from experience, reread Tull's report on Addie's funeral (section 20) and Whitfield's monologue (section 41). Like Whitfield, Cora relies on Biblical injunctions to guide her thinking. As Addie says, she uses words whose meaning she has never experienced and can therefore never truly understand. In sections 2 and 6, and especially in section 39, Cora spouts the empty rhetoric that Addie despises.

13. You can find examples of the conflict between townspeople and country folk throughout the novel. Note Cora's resentment of the way the town lady's canceled orders for cakes dominates her thoughts in section 2. In section 28, Anse complains about "them that runs the stores in the towns . . . living off of them that sweats."

Note also the interaction between the Bundrens and the townspeople. Moseley (section 45) sees Dewey Dell as someone from another world. When the wagon reaches Jefferson (section 52), the conflict nearly turns violent as Jewel reacts with blind rage to what he takes to be an affront to his mother. The conflict extends the theme of isolation amid solidarity by showing that groups of people are separated from one another just as individuals are.

14. Review Peabody's first monologue (section 11) to nail down his view that death is a state of mind—something that affects the thinking of the survivors. Then list the many ways that Addie lives on in her children's and husband's thoughts. The promise she made Anse give dictates the novel's action—the arduous journey to Jefferson. Jewel and Darl continue their sibling rivalry even after Addie's death. Jewel sacrifices his horse for his mother's wish. Vardaman gropes for a reason for her absence and decides she has changed into a fish. Only Cash and Dewey Dell have no obsession with her memory. Yet Cash suffers a broken leg for her. Dewey Dell is too self-absorbed to express any feelings for her mother's death after her anguished outburst at Addie's deathbed (section 12). Yet she too endures the hardships of the journey to get her mother's corpse to Jefferson.

Test 2

1. C   **2.** B   **3.** A   **4.** C   **5.** B   **6.** A

7. C   **8.** C   **9.** B   **10.** C

11. In *As I Lay Dying* the lives of country women are hard, as several characters point out. (See especially Peabody, section 11, and Rachel Samson, section 29.) Faulkner makes us care about all the women in the novel, even the most comic or fatuous of them, like Cora Tull, and even Addie and Dewey Dell in their vengeful moods.

These women are not simple creatures. Faulkner makes them as complex as any of the men, who inhabit different worlds than the women—a fact reinforced by the bewilderment with which Tull, Samson, and Armstid confront their wives.

But women—especially Dewey Dell and Addie—represent an elemental life force. In different ways, they represent fertility, the earth, motherhood. Some readers feel that Addie, Dewey Dell, and Cora, taken together, are meant to represent Persephone, the goddess of spring (new life) and thus of fertility, and queen of the underworld. (Cora's name is derived from Kore, another name for Persephone.) Dewey Dell's name identifies her with the earth, as does her shape. (See the closing lines of sections 14 and 37.) Try as they might, these women cannot alter their roles as earth mothers.

12. Faulkner uses ancient myth as a backdrop to his story in order (1) to suggest a mythic dimension to his characters' lives and actions, (2) to provide a yardstick to measure their actions with, and (3) to provide clues to his characters' natures.

The mythic dimension is suggested by the novel's title, from Homer's *Odyssey*, which brings to mind Odysseus's epic journey and indicates there may be more to the Bundrens' funeral cortege than meets the eye. Odysseus visited Agamemnon in Hades, where the dead king complained about his wife's scorn for him as he lay dying "on the road to Hades' house." Faulkner suggests also that the Bundrens' farm is a sort of sulfurous underworld (sections 10, 14, 17). Later (section 33) there are hints that the swollen and menacing Yoknapatawpha River is an obstacle separating the land of the living from the land of the dead, much like the River Styx. Is Addie then a symbol of fertility, a sort of Persephone—queen of the underworld who left Hades every spring to permit flowers to bloom and grain to grow again? Perhaps. Some readers think that Cora, Addie, and Dewey Dell are a composite of Persephone and Demeter, Persephone's mother and another goddess of fertility. However, the end of Addie's journey is simply another "underworld"—the cemetery in Jefferson. So, in the end, Faulkner pulls the rug out from under those who think he is simply recycling old myths in modern dress. Still,

he has borrowed some of the trappings of the myth—
the concept of an underworld, of women as symbols of
fertility, of the river as a mythical place—and in so doing
has made his characters and their acts seem "larger than
life."

If reference to myth makes the Bundrens larger than
life, it can also be used as a yardstick to make them seem
smaller than their mythical counterparts. Suppose, as
some readers feel, Addie, Dewey Dell, and Cora are a
composite of the fertility goddesses Demeter and her
daughter, Persephone. Demeter and Persephone were
responsible for giving life to all vegetation. When Persephone was in Hades, held captive by Pluto, no crops
grew, no flowers bloomed. Measured against Demeter's
and Persephone's powers, Addie's powers to create and
sustain life seem puny indeed.

Myth can be used to indicate traits of characters in the
novel. Darl constantly refers to Jewel's wooden fea-
tures—his "wooden" back, his "wooden" face. Some
readers feel that Faulkner is calling attention to Jewel's
Dionysian nature—a mixture of virility and cruelty. (See
note in the discussion of section 1.) In section 3, Faulkner hints that Jewel is at once a centaur (half man, half
horse) and Bellerophon, the rider of the winged horse
Pegasus, who defied the gods. What these references to
three different myths have in common is the message
that Jewel is a godlike, masculine figure who is unpredictable and committed to action.

13. In *As I Lay Dying*, Faulkner treats horror matter-of-
factly. This tactic is so unexpected, even though he uses
it again and again, that the result is invariably comic.
Note Tull's description in section 16 of the way Vardaman bored through the coffin lid into Addie's face. Or
Moseley's account of the way the women of Mottson
scattered when confronted with the stench of Addie's

putrifying body (section 45). The total effect is of American folk humor. *As I Lay Dying* has much in common with the tall tale. (See discussion of section 16.)

Another type of humor Faulkner uses frequently is irony—saying one thing and meaning another. Irony takes many forms in *As I Lay Dying*. MacGowan (section 55) thinks he's quite a sophisticated rogue, but his poor grammar, undemanding job, and fear of getting caught mark him for what he is—a small-town wise guy. Anse chastises his sons for behavior disrespectful to Addie's memory, while he can't wait to reach Jefferson, buy some teeth, and get a new wife. Even some of the references to Greek and Biblical myth are ironic. Anse likens himself to Job—a most laughable comparison. If Addie is Persephone, Anse is Pluto—the lord of the underworld, who took Persephone prisoner. A less likely god than this lazy peasant is hard to imagine.

14. Reread sections 32 and 40 to see why Jewel was Addie's burden. As Addie's son by Whitfield, Jewel was living proof of her sin, forcing her to do what she hated most of all—lie. Because of him, she had Dewey Dell and Vardaman in order to make amends to Anse. Jewel was a difficult child, too. But the most crushing blow of all was the rejection she felt when he bought his horse.

He became her "salvation" after her death in two spectacular scenes (sections 36 and 50). He also sacrificed his most prized possession, his horse, for the mules that pulled her corpse to Jefferson.

Term Paper Ideas and other Topics for Writing

Literary Topics

1. Write about *As I Lay Dying* as a tragicomedy—a work of art that combines elements of tragedy and comedy, and usually ends happily.

2. In what ways is *As I Lay Dying* an extended tall tale? Note how it fits into the tradition of American folk humor.

3. Explain how *As I Lay Dying* is a tour de force—a work of art that allows the writer to show off his technical expertise? Give specific examples.

4. Demonstrate how Faulkner's mastery of the folk idiom—the way country folk talk—adds to the humor, pathos, and believability of the novel, and to the reader's enjoyment of it.

The Characters

1. Discuss the novel as a portrait of a failed marriage and its consequences. Compare Anse and Addie's marriage to those of the Armstids, Samsons, and Tulls.

2. Contrast Jewel's bent toward action with Anse's ineffectual reliance on words. Use specific examples.

3. Write Addie's biography in the form of a newspaper obituary, listing her accomplishments as well as her disappointments. Note also her philosophy of life and the part it played in guiding her thoughts and actions.

4. Compare the characters and actions of Cora, Dewey Dell, and Addie with those of the fertility goddesses Demeter and Persephone. Show where the stories merge and where they part.

5. Explain how Faulkner elicits sympathy for characters who most people would recoil from in real life.

The Themes

1. Discuss the novel as a portrait of a family under stress. Note, with examples, what that stress is, and how it forces the Bundrens to reveal themselves.

2. Discuss five major themes of *As I Lay Dying* and explain why readers so often disagree over the novel's meaning. Note the role the book's structure plays in permitting alternative interpretations.

3. "[Man's] tragedy," Faulkner once said, "is the impossibility—or at least the tremendous difficulty—of communication." Demonstrate how *As I Lay Dying* supports this view.

Structure and Style

1. Faulkner does not tell his story in strict chronological order. Explain what this book gains by his refusal to present events in the order in which they happened. Give specific examples.

2. Compare the language and imagery in Jewel's monologue (section 4) with the language and imagery in Dewey Dell's third monologue (section 30). How are they alike? How are they different?

3. Discuss Faulkner's use of objective correlatives—objects, situations, or chains of events that suggest particular emotions. Note his use of animals, dreams, myths, and recalled experience, among other things, as objective correlatives.

Further Reading
CRITICAL WORKS

Backman, Melvin. *Faulkner: The Major Years*. Blooming-
ton: Indiana University Press, 1966.

Barth, J. Robert. *Religious Perspectives in Faulkner's Fiction*.
Notre Dame: University of Notre Dame Press, 1972.

Blotner, Joseph. *Faulkner: A Biography*. New York: Random House, 1984.

Brooks, Cleanth. *William Faulkner: The Yoknapatawpha
Country*. New Haven: Yale University Press, 1963.

Collins, Carvel. "The Pairing of *The Sound and the Fury*
and *As I Lay Dying*," *Princeton University Library Chron-
icle*, XVII (1957), 114–123.

Dickerson, Mary Jane. "Some Sources of Faulkner's Myth
in *As I Lay Dying*," *Mississippi Quarterly*, XIX (1966),
132–142.

Howe, Irving. *William Faulkner: A Critical Study*. Chicago:
University of Chicago Press, 1975.

Millgate, Michael. *The Achievement of William Faulkner*.
Lincoln: University of Nebraska Press, 1978.

Ross, Stephen M. " 'Voice' in Narrative Texts: The Example of *As I Lay Dying*," *PMLA*, 94 (March 1979),
300–310.

Schmitter, Dean Morgan. *William Faulkner*. New York:
McGraw Hill, 1973.

Thompson, Lawrence. *William Faulkner: An Introduction
and Interpretation*. New York: Barnes & Noble, 1963.

Vickery, Olga W. *The Novels of William Faulkner: A Critical
Interpretation*. Baton Rouge: Louisiana State University
Press, 1964.

AUTHOR'S OTHER MAJOR WORKS
Novels

1926	Soldiers' Pay	1942	Go Down, Moses
1927	Mosquitoes	1948	Intruder in the Dust
1929	Sartoris	1951	Requiem for a Nun
1929	The Sound and the Fury		(partly a play)
1931	Sanctuary	1954	A Fable
1932	Light in August	1957	The Town
1935	Pylon	1959	The Mansion
1936	Absalom, Absalom!	1962	The Reivers
1938	The Unvanquished	1973	Flags in the Dust
1939	The Wild Palms		(uncut version
1940	The Hamlet		of Sartoris)

Story Collections

1931   These 13
1934   Doctor Martino and Other Stories
1949   Knight's Gambit (The title story, the length of a short novel, is sometimes counted as a novel.)
1950   Collected Stories
1955   Big Woods
1979   Uncollected Stories of William Faulkner

The Critics
Old Testament Vision

Nothing so permeates the tone and texture of the story as does the spirit of the Old Testament. The themes, the attitudes, and frequently the very words and prose rhythms derive from the written account of the "pre-Christian" experience. Specifically, the story as a whole has strong overtones of the Book of Job. Salvation, religiosity, tribal solidarity, the importance of sex as an almost religious act—these and other Old Testament themes assert themselves. . . . Above all, there is the brooding Old Testament spirit of despair, hope, endurance—tensions as old as mankind—with which man faces the darkness and mystery of the world around him.

>   —Philip C. Rule, "The Old
>   Testament Vision in *As I Lay
>   Dying*," in *Religious Perspectives
>   in Faulkner's Fiction*, 1972

Tour de Force

The use of a wide range of viewpoints gives moral as well as narrative perspective, offers scope for rich ironic effects, and broadens the sense of social reality. . . . The technique of the novel represents, of course, a *tour de force* of conception as well as of execution, and in his determination to avoid any authorial intrusion Faulkner perhaps allowed a certain dilution of the tensions arising from the internal psychological dramas of his major characters . . . On the other hand, the book as it stands offers a vivid evocation of the widening circle of impact of the Bundrens' adventure, an effect which harmonises with the circular and radiating techniques of the book as a whole and with its recurring images of the circle, from the circling buzzards to the wheels of the wagon itself.

>   —Michael Millgate, *The
>   Achievement of William Faulkner*,
>   1978

A Dissenting Opinion

After the reader has marveled at Faulkner's experimentations in *As I Lay Dying*, there is no need to be stricken into critical silence by it. The total effect is disappointing; the inadequacy of the characterizations fails to arouse our sympathies and compassions; the ending makes us feel as though we had been tricked into caring at all; the artistry seems glib when compared with the uses of the same technical procedures in [Faulkner's] *The Sound and the Fury;* and the total idea moves us even less than the total action. . . . *As I Lay Dying* has been too highly praised by too many critics.

>   —Lawrance Thompson, *William
>   Faulkner: An Introduction and
>   Interpretation*, 1963

Levels of Consciousness

. . . [Each] private world manifests a fixed and distinctive way of reacting to and ordering experience. Words, action, and contemplation constitute the possible modes of response, while sensation, reason, and intuition form the levels of consciousness. All of these combine to establish a total relationship between the individual and his experience; for certain of the characters in *As I Lay Dying*, however, this relationship is fragmented and distorted. Anse, for example, is always a bystander, contemplating events and reducing the richness of the experience to a few threadbare clichés. In contrast, Darl, the most complex of the characters, owes his complexity and his madness to the fact that he encompasses all possible modes of response and awareness without being able to effect their integration. It is Cash, the oldest brother, who ultimately achieves maturity and understanding by integrating these modes into one distinctively human response which fuses words and action, reason and intuition. In short, the Bundren family provides a locus for the exploration of the human psyche in all its complexity. . . .

—Olga W. Vickery, *The Novels of
William Faulkner*, 1964

Testing Addie's Children

As I Lay Dying is a fable not only about Addie's quest for salvation but about the testing of three sons by the ordeals of water and fire. Their crossing of the flooded river with the mother's corpse is the first test. . . . Darl came out of the water with empty hands, Cash with the horse (the substitute for the mother), and Jewel with the prize—the coffin. The rescue of the coffin may be interpreted in two ways: it signifies the living mother that Jewel saves, and it signifies the love that Jewel retains. Cash and Jewel sacrificed what they loved: Cash his tools, Jewel his horse. Cash's sacrifice was returned, but Jewel's was accepted. Darl had nothing to sacrifice.

—Melvin Backman, *Faulkner: The
Major Years*, 1966